LIVING YOUR STRENGTHS

*Discover your God-given talents
and inspire your community*

LIVING YOUR STRENGTHS

*Discover your God-given talents
and inspire your community*

**Albert L. Winseman, D.Min.
Donald O. Clifton, Ph.D.
Curt Liesveld, M.Div.**

Gallup Press
New York

Gallup Press
1251 Avenue of the Americas
23rd Floor
New York, NY 10020

Manufactured in the United States of America

Second edition 2004

10 9 8 7 6 5

Library of Congress Control Number: 2004107418

ISBN: 1-59562-002-8

For my wife Jane:
You are and always will be
the love of my life and my greatest source of strength.
—Albert L. Winseman

To Shirley, my wife of 57 years, who has helped our
four children live their strengths.
—Donald O. Clifton

To my wife Rosanne:
Our marriage will always be my greatest success.
Your loving partnership continues to bring out the best of
what God has put in me.
—Curt Liesveld

We also dedicate this book to our coauthor, Don Clifton, who passed away in September 2003. Don's lifelong belief that people are at their best when they maximize their strengths, rather than try to fix their weaknesses, has inspired more than one million people to discover their talents and begin to live their strengths. We are deeply grateful to Don for the way he touched our lives.

— Al and Curt

TABLE OF CONTENTS

INTRODUCTION

American churches are experiencing a power shortage. It's not the kind of power shortage that can be fixed by opening natural gas fields or drilling oil wells or building electrical plants. The shortage is in fulfilled human potential. In churches all across the United States, people aren't harnessing the power of their innate gifts. They are not fulfilling God's purpose in their lives. And most people don't even know it.

The Gallup Organization's 2002 national study of congregation members uncovered the roots of this problem. It revealed that most people (53%) do not strongly agree with the statement "In my congregation, I regularly have the opportunity to do what I do best." Clearly, too many individuals' talents and strengths are going unrecognized and unappreciated. And this adds up to an enormous loss of human potential that could be tapped for the transformation of society.

We need a revolution in our churches — a strengths revolution. This book was written to get that revolution started.

THE FOLLY OF "WEAKNESS PREVENTION"

If you're like most people, you have grown up with the "weakness prevention" model. You've been told that to become strong, successful, or truly serve God and the world, you must "fix" your weaknesses. You've been told that your talents and strengths are a source of sinful pride. (Many of you confess every Sunday to being "miserable offenders" and to a host of other inadequacies!) What you really need to do, the "weakness experts" say, is to develop your areas of *non-talent*. Then, they believe, you will be ready to fully serve God and the world.

That thinking is just plain wrong.

In Gallup's research into human potential over the past 30 years — including interviews with more than 2 million people — the evidence is overwhelming: You will be most successful in whatever you do by building your life around your greatest natural abilities rather than your weaknesses. *Your talents should be your primary focus!* The problem is that most people don't even know what their greatest talents are or how to go about discovering them. This book will help you do that.

As you read this book, remember that God has given you a unique combination of talents. God also places within you a calling — a calling to serve others and advance the cause of Christ and the Church, a calling to ministry. Your calling is what God wants you to do with your life; your talents and strengths determine how you will get it done. When you discover your talents, you begin to discover your calling.

Like everyone, God has blessed you with a deep reservoir of untapped potential. That potential is your talent, waiting to be discovered and put to use in your life. It's time for you to unleash the power of that potential and begin to discover your unique talents.

Start by taking Gallup's Clifton StrengthsFinder, an online talent assessment instrument. You'll find instructions on how to take the Clifton StrengthsFinder on the following page. Then get ready to embark on an adventure sure to change your life.

Take the Clifton StrengthsFinder

Your ID code is located on the reverse side of the jacket of this book. We recommend that before you begin to read this book, you use your ID code to log on to the Clifton StrengthsFinder Web site and take the assessment.

GO TO:

https://sf1.strengthsfinder.com/

Minimum system requirements for the Clifton StrengthsFinder Web site:

- 33.6K modem (56K modem or faster recommended)
- Internet Explorer 5.5+ or Firefox 1.0+

ANY QUESTIONS?
If you have any questions or difficulties regarding the Gallup Clifton StrengthsFinder Web site, please feel free to e-mail Gallup Client Support at **help@strengthsfinder.com** or call **1-800-818-6979** (toll free in the United States) or **1-402-486-6800**.

CHAPTER 1

The Power of the Right Fit

To understand how churches often fail to tap the natural abilities of their congregants, consider the story of Liz and Rick.

A married couple in their early thirties, Liz and Rick moved to a new city, and after several months of searching, found a congregation to join. They went through new-member orientation and told the coordinator that they wanted to get involved in the church. They weren't quite sure what they wanted to do, but they knew they wanted to do a lot more than just attend services.

A few weeks after they joined, they got a call from the new-member coordinator asking them if they would be greeters for services during July. Rick and Liz agreed and dutifully showed up to shake hands with congregants for five Sundays in July.

The couple had almost diametrically opposed reactions to the experience. "I loved it!" recalls Liz. "This was great. I like meeting new people, and being a greeter made me feel like I was making a contribution to my congregation. I'd do it every week if I could!"

But Rick's reaction was not so positive. He remembers, "It was like pulling teeth. I was really uncomfortable. I didn't know what to say or what to do. It doesn't come naturally for me like it does for Liz. I guess I'm just shy by nature. I sure hope no one asks me to do this again."

By asking Rick and Liz to serve as greeters, the new-member coordinator was subscribing to the myth that "an active member is a faithful member." The coordinator must have thought, "Anybody can be a greeter. After all, it's a great way to get to know the members of the congregation." So she asked Liz and Rick to fill roles in the congregation without first discovering their natural abilities — their talents. She lucked out with Liz, who will likely become more engaged by the experience. But if she continues to ask Rick to be a greeter, he will become disengaged very quickly.

Why did Liz and Rick react differently? Because Liz loves to meet new people and to win them over. In her world, there are no strangers, just new friends she hasn't met. So being a greeter fits naturally with Liz's innate abilities. Rick, in contrast, doesn't want to meet and greet a stream of people. It makes him uncomfortable and doesn't come naturally to him. Rick would rather deepen existing relationships than form a bunch of new ones.

Rick's predicament is all too familiar in churches across the country. How about you? Have you found your "place" in your church? Do you have the opportunity in your church to do what you do best on a regular basis — to use your talents and strengths? Do you find joy, satisfaction, and growth in the ways that you serve God, your church, and other people?

If you answered "no" to any or all of these questions, read on! Your life at church — not to mention your personal, family, or professional life — could be a lot more fulfilling. The first step is defining what a strength is — and what it is not.

WHAT IS A STRENGTH?

To begin to know and live your strengths, you need to understand what a strength is. A **strength** is the ability to provide consistent, near-perfect performance in a given activity. This ability is a powerful, productive combination of talent, skill, and knowledge.

To better understand what a strength looks like, consider Steve, who for the past 20 years has been teaching Bible studies at his church. His classes are always among the most popular offered by his church, and he often draws a standing-room-only crowd. "I got started doing this by volunteering to teach a six-week class on the Gospel of Mark during Lent one year," he recalls. "I teach training classes at work, and I thought I'd give it a shot. I loved it! Even though that first class went well, I knew I wanted to get a lot better at it."

Over the years, Steve has audited classes at the Bible college in his community, taught himself elementary Greek and Hebrew, subscribed to a biblical archaeology magazine, and learned to do multimedia presentations to enhance his lessons. "I'm a much better teacher than I was 20 years ago. It's definitely been worth the effort." Steve started out with some natural talents for teaching, and by adding skills and knowledge, he built those talents into a strength.

The key to building a strength is to first identify your dominant themes of talent, then delve into those themes to identify a specific talent, and finally produce a strength by refining that talent with knowledge and skill.

Talents are naturally recurring patterns of thought, feeling, or behavior that can be productively applied. Unlike skills and knowledge, talents naturally exist within you and cannot be acquired. They are your inborn predispositions. They are the things that you do instinctively and that naturally give you satisfaction. Your spontaneous, top-of-mind reactions to the situations you encounter are the best indicators of your talents. Everyone is talented, but we recognize some people's talents more easily than others — simply because these people are in roles that they consistently perform with excellence and because the roles are suited to their natural predispositions.

What does a talent look like? A talent can be the natural tendency to:

- be competitive
- pick up on the emotions of others
- thrive under pressure
- make others laugh
- enjoy puzzles
- recognize the uniqueness in others
- envision and clearly articulate a future scenario

Skills are the abilities to perform the steps of an activity. Your skills show your competence when proceeding through the "how to's" of a task; they reflect your rational and predictable areas of expertise. Skills can be learned. Once you've acquired the skills necessary for a given activity, you have the ability to perform its basic steps.

What does a skill look like? A skill can be the ability to perform the basic steps of:

- adding and subtracting
- processing a customer's insurance claim
- using software to prepare a presentation
- giving a patient an injection
- parallel parking
- preparing a lesson plan
- checking someone into a hotel

Knowledge is, simply, what you know. You can acquire knowledge through education or training. It may be factual knowledge, like the words of a foreign language, the books of the Bible, software features, or the table of periodic elements. It also may be experiential knowledge, which isn't taught in classrooms or in manuals. Experiential knowledge includes the insights or awareness you have gained through experience.

What does knowledge look like? Your knowledge could tell you:

- how to deal with an upset customer
- how to cope with job-related stress
- what time weekend services are held at your church
- the FAA's safety regulations
- what part of a lesson your students find most difficult
- the fastest route to the grocery store
- why and how Martin Luther started the Protestant Reformation

An important difference between talents and skills and knowledge is that although skills and knowledge can be acquired, their applicability is restricted because they can be very situation-specific. Just because an individual is a successful accountant doesn't mean that person could also be a successful heart surgeon. The skills and knowledge needed for accounting are very different from those needed for heart surgery. However, given enough time, commitment, and opportunity to learn, an accountant could learn the skills necessary to be a heart surgeon, and vice versa. But talents are a different story. Without possessing the talents for those activities, the heart surgeon could not *excel* as an accountant, and the accountant could not *excel* as a heart surgeon.

Talents are transferable from situation to situation. The hotel desk clerk who instinctively knows just the right way to make a guest feel welcome and at home would most likely be an excellent greeter for worship services at his or her church. Skills and knowledge can be acquired, but they will not significantly help you unless they enhance a talent.

The apostle Paul is a perfect example of someone whose talents remain constant in different situations. Before his conversion on the road to Damascus (Acts 9), Paul — who was then known as Saul — was stubborn, single-minded, and zealous in his attacks on Christians. After his conversion, Paul was stubborn, single-minded, and zealous in his defense of Christianity. His conversion did not change his talents. What changed for Paul as a result of his conversion were his *values*. After his encounter with the risen Christ, instead of using his talents to hunt and persecute Christians in an effort to destroy the Church, Paul was using those same talents to seek and convert non-Christians with the intent of growing the Church. The same talents that made him such a formidable enemy of the Church were now making him its invaluable champion.

The fundamental building block of any strength is talent. When you enhance a talent by adding the right skills and useful knowledge, you have created a strength. Again, to live your strengths, you must first identify your talents. By taking the Clifton StrengthsFinder, you identified your top five themes of talent—your "Signature Themes."

A THEOLOGY OF STRENGTHS

There is something about the concept of talents and strengths that just "feels right." When we discover our talents, when we give them a name, something resonates deep within us. It is as if our spirits react to this discovery with a resounding "Yes! This is the way it is supposed to be — this is who I was created to be." And we find it somehow freeing; naming our greatest talents sets us free to develop them and live through them. Naming our top talents gives us permission to accept our areas of lesser talent and either discard them or manage them. It gives us permission to stop trying to be who we are not and concentrate on who we are — who we were originally created to be.

The Judeo-Christian tradition affirms what we already know in our souls. Consider these passages from the Old and New Testaments:

- The first creation story in Genesis, the first book of the Old Testament, depicts a scene of beauty, serenity, and goodness. The crowning achievement of Creation was humankind:

So God created humankind in his image,
  in the image of God he created them;
  male and female he created them . . .
God saw everything that he had made, and indeed, it was very good.
Genesis 1:27, 31a

- In the book of Jeremiah in the Old Testament, we find this:

Now the word of the LORD came to me saying,
  "Before I formed you in the womb I knew you,
  and before you were born I consecrated you;
  I appointed you a prophet to the nations."
Jeremiah 1:4-5

- In his first letter to the Corinthians, the apostle Paul points out that members of the Church each have different gifts and talents, which are to be used for the good of the entire Church:

Now there are varieties of gifts, but the same Spirit; and there are varieties of services, but the same Lord; and there are varieties of activities, but it is the same God who activates all of them in everyone. To each is given the manifestation of the Spirit for the common good ... All these are activated by one and the same Spirit, who allots to each one individually just as the Spirit chooses.
1 Corinthians 12:14-20

From a spiritual viewpoint, when we deny our talents and instead focus on our weaknesses, on some level, we are telling God that we know best and that God somehow made a mistake in gracing us with our unique mix of talents.

Consider the Hasidic tale of the Rabbi Zusya. When he was an old man, Zusya said, "In the coming world, they will not ask me: 'Why were you not Moses?' They will ask me: 'Why were you not Zusya?'"[1] That is God's question to each of us as well. We are not expected to be who we are *not*. We are expected to be who we *are*.

We hope that this book will help you discover and affirm your areas of greatest talent and help you discover ways to live through your God-given talents in your congregation, as well as in your personal and professional life. At the very least, we hope that when you finish this book, your active involvement in your church won't be frustrating like Rick's, but as fulfilling and inspiring as Liz's. Only by knowing your talents and strengths and by living through them can you be the best *you* that you can be.

---

[1] Martin Buber, *Tales of the Hasidim: The Early Masters* (New York: Schocken Books, 1975), p. 251.

CHAPTER 2

Identifying and Affirming
Your Talents

At an early age, you started hearing it: It's a virtue to be "well-rounded." You were told this was your ticket to teachers' approval, straight A's, a great college, a successful career — not to mention money, happiness, and fulfillment. Through schooling, training, and societal expectations, you got the message: Soften your sharp edges. Become smooth and well-rounded. (They might as well have said: Become as dull as you possibly can be.)

Here's the problem: Conventional wisdom doesn't consider who you really are. And, besides, *God didn't make you well-rounded!*

Why don't you start, right now, to defy that "wisdom" — and begin appreciating your unique, God-given talents? Individuals become strong by focusing on those unique talents to develop and apply their strengths.

When we focus on our talents, we are more effective at our tasks and roles. We are also more successful, happy, and fulfilled. Just ask Bill. Reflecting on his years as a pastor, Bill realized that even though public speaking didn't come naturally to him, he nevertheless was an effective preacher because he focused on his talents. "The times I seemed to get the most positive feedback on my sermons were the times I was able to link a concept with a personal story — when I was able to be the most authentic or transparent as a person," he says.

Bill was able to do this because of his talents in Relator, one of his Signature Themes. (We will discuss the specifics of Relator and the other 33 themes later in this chapter.) "Relators want to be real; they want to be authentic; they want to be themselves," Bill says. "I was pretty comfortable doing that, even in front of a bunch of people. Now, these were obviously people that I knew pretty well, and so I was willing to let them know who I was. I think it helped me be a better communicator sometimes. Even though I wasn't a natural communicator in front of people, I think it was my Relator and maybe my Learner talents that helped me to do that. I like to learn stuff and then make it real through my own stories."

Just as Bill's greatest talents did for him, your dominant natural responses will determine how you approach a challenge, relate to others, and fulfill God's purpose for your life.

By now, you should have taken the Clifton StrengthsFinder assessment and learned your Signature Themes. (If you haven't taken the assessment, take it now before you read on.) The theme descriptions, Scripture passages, and insights that follow are intended to help you recognize and affirm your talents in these themes and increase your awareness that your talents are not only a gift from God, they are also the foundation on which you can excel and lead a fulfilling life through strengths.

ACHIEVER

Your Achiever theme helps explain your drive. Achiever describes a constant need for achievement. You feel as if every day starts at zero. By the end of the day you must achieve something tangible in order to feel good about yourself. And by "every day" you mean every single day — workdays, weekends, vacations. No matter how much you may feel you deserve a day of rest, if the day passes without some form of achievement, no matter how small, you will feel dissatisfied. You have an internal fire burning inside you. It pushes you to do more, to achieve more. After each accomplishment is reached, the fire dwindles for a moment, but very soon it rekindles itself, forcing you toward the next accomplishment. Your relentless need for achievement might not be logical. It might not even be focused. But it will always be with you. As an Achiever you must learn to live with this whisper of discontent. It does have its benefits. It brings you the energy you need to work long hours without burning out. It is the jolt you can always count on to get you started on new tasks, new challenges. It is the power supply that causes you to set the pace and define the levels of productivity for your workgroup. It is the theme that keeps you moving.

Scriptures that relate to the Achiever theme:

What good is it, my brothers and sisters, if you say you have faith but do not have works? Can faith save you? If a brother or sister is naked and lacks daily food, and one of you says to them, "Go in peace; keep warm and eat your fill," and yet you do not supply their bodily needs, what is the good of that? So faith by itself, if it has no works, is dead.

James 2:14-17

But we appeal to you, brothers and sisters, to respect those who labor among you, and have charge of you in the Lord and admonish you; esteem them very highly in love because of their work.

1 Thessalonians 5:12-13

One who is slack in work
*   is close kin to a vandal.*

Proverbs 18:9

And we want each one of you to show the same diligence so as to realize the full assurance of hope to the very end, so that you may not become sluggish, but imitators of those who through faith and patience inherit the promises.

Hebrews 6:11-12

For further understanding of your talents, examine these five insights and select those that describe you best.

- ☐ You work very hard to complete each task on your "to do" list, and you always have a long list of things to do.

- ☐ You are busy and productive, and you derive satisfaction from your accomplishments.

- ☐ You have a great deal of stamina and determination to achieve your goals.

- ☐ Other people may criticize you, because to them you seem too driven to achieve. They may call you a "workaholic," but the truth is that you like your work, and you like to work hard.

☐ Achiever talents are valuable because they help you remain motivated to reach your goals and to push for higher and higher levels of excellence. You won't rest until you reach your most highly desired goals — and they must be *your* goals.

ACTIVATOR

"When can we start?" This is a recurring question in your life. You are impatient for action. You may concede that analysis has its uses or that debate and discussion can occasionally yield some valuable insights, but deep down you know that only action is real. Only action can make things happen. Only action leads to performance. Once a decision is made, you cannot not act. Others may worry that "there are still some things we don't know," but this doesn't seem to slow you. If the decision has been made to go across town, you know that the fastest way to get there is to go stoplight to stoplight. You are not going to sit around waiting until all the lights have turned green. Besides, in your view, action and thinking are not opposites. In fact, guided by your Activator theme, you believe that action is the best device for learning. You make a decision, you take action, you look at the result, and you learn. This learning informs your next action and your next. How can you grow if you have nothing to react to? Well, you believe you can't. You must put yourself out there. You must take the next step. It is the only way to keep your thinking fresh and informed. The bottom line is this: You know you will be judged not by what you say, not by what you think, but by what you get done. This does not frighten you. It pleases you.

Scriptures that relate to the Activator theme:

But be doers of the word, and not merely hearers who deceive themselves. For if any are hearers of the word and not doers, they are like those who look at themselves in a mirror; for they look at themselves and, on going away, immediately forget what they were like.
James 1:22-24

Whoever observes the wind will not sow;
*   and whoever regards the clouds will not reap.*
Just as you do not know how the breath comes to the bones in the mother's womb, so you do not know the work of God, who makes everything.

In the morning sow your seed, and at evening do not let your hands be idle; for you do not know which will prosper, this or that, or whether both alike will be good.
Ecclesiastes 11:4-6

If you know these things, you are blessed if you do them.
John 13:17

For further understanding of your talents, examine these five insights and select those that describe you best.

- ☐ You can see how ideas can be turned into action.
- ☐ You want to do things now, rather than simply talk about doing them.
- ☐ You can be very powerful in making things happen and getting other people to take action.
- ☐ Other people may criticize you for being impatient and seeming to "run over" them. You will probably struggle with people who try to control you.
- ☐ Activator talents are valuable because they generate the energy to get things going and then done. This theme brings innovation and creative approaches to problem solving.

ADAPTABILITY

You live in the moment. You don't see the future as a fixed destination. Instead, you see it as a place that you create out of the choices that you make right now. And so you discover your future one choice at a time. This doesn't mean that you don't have plans. You probably do. But this theme of Adaptability does enable you to respond willingly to the demands of the moment even if they pull you away from your plans. Unlike some, you don't resent sudden requests or unforeseen detours. You expect them. They are inevitable. Indeed, on some level you actually look forward to them. You are, at heart, a very flexible person who can stay productive when the demands of work are pulling you in many different directions at once.

Scriptures that relate to the Adaptability theme:

So do not worry about tomorrow, for tomorrow will bring worries of its own. Today's trouble is enough for today.
Matthew 6:34

People were bringing little children to him in order that he might touch them; and the disciples spoke sternly to them. But when Jesus saw this, he was indignant and said to them, "Let the little children come to me; do not stop them; for it is to such as these that the kingdom of God belongs. Truly I tell you, whoever does not receive the kingdom of God as a little child will never enter it." And he took them up in his arms, laid his hands on them, and blessed them.
Mark 10:13-16

When Jesus came to the place, he looked up and said to him, "Zacchaeus, hurry and come down; for I must stay at your house today." So he hurried down and was happy to welcome him. All who saw it began to grumble and said, "He has gone to be the guest of one who is a sinner." Zacchaeus stood there and said to the Lord, "Look, half of my possessions, Lord, I will give to the poor; and if I have defrauded anyone of anything, I will pay back four times as much." Then Jesus said to him, "Today salvation has come to this house, because he too is a son of Abraham."

Luke 19:5-9

I know what it is to have little, and I know what it is to have plenty. In any and all circumstances I have learned the secret of being well-fed and of going hungry, of having plenty and of being in need. I can do all things through him who strengthens me.

Philippians 4:12-13

For further understanding of your talents, examine these five insights and select those that describe you best.

☐ You can modify yourself depending on the demands in your environment.

☐ You adjust to many things all day long because you live in the moment.

☐ You create and discover the future out of the choices you make right now, one choice at a time.

☐ Your "go with the flow" attitude may seem like irresponsibility to those who like structure and predictability.

☐ Adaptability talents are valuable because they allow you to keep moving forward when the unexpected happens.

You can move ahead in a world of unknowns and seemingly unfair treatment when others would give up. You can deal with everything from injustices to crises and still find a way to make progress.

ANALYTICAL

Your Analytical theme challenges other people: "Prove it. Show me why what you are claiming is true." In the face of this kind of questioning some will find that their brilliant theories wither and die. For you, this is precisely the point. You do not necessarily want to destroy other people's ideas, but you do insist that their theories be sound. You see yourself as objective and dispassionate. You like data because they are value free. They have no agenda. Armed with these data, you search for patterns and connections. You want to understand how certain patterns affect one another. How do they combine? What is their outcome? Does this outcome fit with the theory being offered or the situation being confronted? These are your questions. You peel the layers back until, gradually, the root cause or causes are revealed. Others see you as logical and rigorous. Over time they will come to you in order to expose someone's "wishful thinking" or "clumsy thinking" to your refining mind. It is hoped that your analysis is never delivered too harshly. Otherwise, others may avoid you when that "wishful thinking" is their own.

Scriptures that relate to the Analytical theme:

But Thomas (who was called the Twin), one of the twelve, was not with them when Jesus came. So the other disciples told him, "We have seen the Lord." But he said to them, "Unless I see the mark of the nails in his hands, and put my finger in the mark of the nails and my hand in his side, I will not believe."
John 20:24-25

These Jews were more receptive than those in Thessalonica, for they welcomed the message very eagerly and examined the scriptures every day to see whether these things were so.
Acts 17:11

"Give your servant therefore an understanding mind to govern your people, able to discern between good and evil; for who can govern this your great people?" It pleased the Lord that Solomon had asked this. God said to him, "Because you have asked this, and have not asked for yourself long life or riches, or for the life of your enemies, but have asked for yourself understanding to discern what is right, I now do according to your word. Indeed I give you a wise and discerning mind; no one like you has been before you and no one like you shall arise after you."
1 Kings 3:9-12

For further understanding of your talents, examine these five insights and select those that describe you best.

☐ You search for the reasons why things are the way they are.

☐ You think about the factors that might affect a situation and what causes certain reactions.

☐ You are critical about why people may claim something is true and want to see the proof.

☐ Some people may reject you and your questioning ways because you insist that the facts are verifiable, theories are sound, and reasoning is logical. Some people may think you are negative or unnecessarily critical when, from your standpoint, you are simply trying to understand something.

☐ Analytical talents are valuable because they enable you to dig deep, find the root causes and effects, and then develop clear thoughts about what is true. This type of thinking helps you become clearer about what excellence is and how it can be attained.

ARRANGER

You are a conductor. When faced with a complex situation involving many factors, you enjoy managing all of the variables, aligning and realigning them until you are sure you have arranged them in the most productive configuration possible. In your mind there is nothing special about what you are doing. You are simply trying to figure out the best way to get things done. But others, lacking this theme, will be in awe of your ability. "How can you keep so many things in your head at once?" they will ask. "How can you stay so flexible, so willing to shelve well-laid plans in favor of some brand-new configuration that has just occurred to you?" But you cannot imagine behaving in any other way. You are a shining example of effective flexibility, whether you are changing travel schedules at the last minute because a better fare has popped up or mulling over just the right combination of people and resources to accomplish a new project. From the mundane to the complex, you are always looking for the perfect configuration. Of course, you are at your best in dynamic situations. Confronted with the unexpected, some complain that plans devised with such care cannot be changed, while others take refuge in the existing rules or procedures. You don't do either. Instead, you jump into the confusion, devising new options, hunting for new paths of least resistance, and figuring out new partnerships — because, after all, there might just be a better way.

Scriptures that relate to the Arranger theme:

Without counsel, plans go wrong,
but with many advisers they succeed.
Proverbs 15:22

what are human beings that you are mindful of them,
mortals that you care for them?
Yet you have made them a little lower than God,
and crowned them with glory and honor.
You have given them dominion over the works of your hands;
you have put all things under their feet,
Psalm 8:4-6

For further understanding of your talents, examine these five insights and select those that describe you best.

☐ You are highly organized and highly flexible.

☐ You can get a lot done, even though you usually have many projects going at the same time.

☐ You enjoy coordinating all of the complex factors that go into making a project successful.

☐ Some people who like to do things by rules and procedures may find your ways chaotic. They may think that your effectiveness is mystery or pure luck.

☐ Arranger talents are valuable because they help you keep looking for the right combinations of people and resources to complete projects successfully.

BELIEF

If you possess a strong Belief theme, you have certain core values that are enduring. These values vary from one person to another, but ordinarily your Belief theme causes you to be family-oriented, altruistic, even spiritual, and to value responsibility and high ethics — both in yourself and others. These core values affect your behavior in many ways. They give your life meaning and satisfaction; in your view, success is more than money and prestige. They provide you with direction, guiding you through the temptations and distractions of life toward a consistent set of priorities. This consistency is the foundation for all your relationships. Your friends call you dependable. "I know where you stand," they say. Your Belief makes you easy to trust. It also demands that you find work that meshes with your values. Your work must be meaningful; it must matter to you. And guided by your Belief theme it will matter only if it gives you a chance to live out your values.

Scriptures that relate to the Belief theme:

Now if you are unwilling to serve the LORD, choose this day whom you will serve, whether the gods your ancestors served in the region beyond the River or the gods of the Amorites in whose land you are living; but as for me and my household, we will serve the LORD.
Joshua 24:15

Whatever your task, put yourselves into it, as done for the Lord and not for your masters, since you know that from the Lord you will receive the inheritance as your reward; you serve the Lord Christ.

Colossians 3:23-24

Then he said to Thomas, "Put your finger here and see my hands. Reach out your hand and put it in my side. Do not doubt but believe." Thomas answered him, "My Lord and my God!" Jesus said to him, "Have you believed because you have seen me? Blessed are those who have not seen and yet have come to believe."

John 20:27-29

For further understanding of your talents, examine these five insights and select those that describe you best.

- ☐ You have core values that are unchanging. You may conflict with people who oppose or don't value your beliefs.

- ☐ You have deeply held ideas about what is, what should be, and the purpose of your life.

- ☐ You will become energetic about a task, role, or position that promotes one of your deeply held beliefs.

- ☐ Some people may think you are rigid or contrary because of your strongly held beliefs.

- ☐ Belief talents are valuable because they produce the motivation for you to work hard, excel, and achieve, as long as achieving is consistent with your values and beliefs. Your set of beliefs does more than energize you — it is the basis for developing a meaningful life.

COMMAND

Command leads you to take charge. Unlike some people, you feel no discomfort with imposing your views on others. On the contrary, once your opinion is formed, you need to share it with others. Once your goal is set, you feel restless until you have aligned others with you. You are not frightened by confrontation; rather, you know that confrontation is the first step toward resolution. Whereas others may avoid facing up to life's unpleasantness, you feel compelled to present the facts or the truth, no matter how unpleasant it may be. You need things to be clear between people and challenge them to be clear-eyed and honest. You push them to take risks. You may even intimidate them. And while some may resent this, labeling you opinionated, they often willingly hand you the reins. People are drawn toward those who take a stance and ask them to move in a certain direction. Therefore, people will be drawn to you. You have presence. You have Command.

Scriptures that relate to the Command theme:

Making a whip of cords, he drove all of them out of the temple, both the sheep and the cattle. He also poured out the coins of the money changers and overturned their tables. He told those who were selling the doves, "Take these things out of here! Stop making my Father's house a marketplace!" His disciples remembered that it was written, "Zeal for your house will consume me."

John 2:15-17

29

So then, putting away falsehood, let all of us speak the truth to our neighbors, for we are members of one another.
Ephesians 4:25

David said to Saul, "Let no one's heart fail because of him; your servant will go and fight with this Philistine." Saul said to David, "You are not able to go against this Philistine to fight with him; for you are just a boy, and he has been a warrior from his youth." But David said to Saul, "Your servant used to keep sheep for his father; and whenever a lion or a bear came, and took a lamb from the flock, I went after it and struck it down, rescuing the lamb from its mouth; and if it turned against me, I would catch it by the jaw, strike it down, and kill it. Your servant has killed both lions and bears; and this uncircumcised Philistine shall be like one of them, since he has defied the armies of the living God." David said, "The LORD, who saved me from the paw of the lion and from the paw of the bear, will save me from the hand of this Philistine." So Saul said to David, "Go, and may the LORD be with you!"
1 Samuel 17:32-37

For further understanding of your talents, examine these five insights and select those that describe you best.

☐ You see what needs to be done, and you are willing to say so.

☐ You are willing to go into a confrontation and argue because you know that what is right will prevail, and confrontations often help get things moving.

☐ You can jump into a conflict, crisis, or emergency and take charge of the situation.

☐ Other people may be threatened, offended, or put off by the power you can command, but most wish they had some of your talents.

☐ Command talents are valuable because they help you positively impact other people. You can help people and entire organizations get through difficult times and make substantive changes in the midst of chaos.

COMMUNICATION

You like to explain, to describe, to host, to speak in public, and to write. This is your Communication theme at work. Ideas are a dry beginning. Events are static. You feel a need to bring them to life, to energize them, to make them exciting and vivid. And so you turn events into stories and practice telling them. You take the dry idea and enliven it with images and examples and metaphors. You believe that most people have a very short attention span. They are bombarded by information, but very little of it survives. You want your information — whether an idea, an event, a product's features and benefits, a discovery, or a lesson — to survive. You want to divert their attention toward you and then capture it, lock it in. This is what drives your hunt for the perfect phrase. This is what draws you toward dramatic words and powerful word combinations. This is why people like to listen to you. Your word pictures pique their interest, sharpen their world, and inspire them to act.

Scriptures that relate to the Communication theme:

Now when Jesus had finished saying these things, the crowds were astounded at his teaching, for he taught them as one having authority, and not as their scribes.
Matthew 7:28-29

Jesus told the crowds all these things in parables; without a parable he told them nothing.
Matthew 13:34

Besides being wise, the Teacher also taught the people knowledge, weighing and studying and arranging many proverbs. The Teacher sought to find pleasing words, and he wrote words of truth plainly.

The sayings of the wise are like goads, and like nails firmly fixed are the collected sayings that are given by one shepherd.
Ecclesiastes 12:9-11

But how are they to call on one in whom they have not believed? And how are they to believe in one of whom they have never heard? And how are they to hear without someone to proclaim him? And how are they to proclaim him unless they are sent? As it is written, "How beautiful are the feet of those who bring good news!"
Romans 10:14-15

For further understanding of your talents, examine these five insights and select those that describe you best.

☐ You like to talk, and you are good at it.

☐ You can explain things and make them clear.

☐ You may have an ability to tell particularly captivating stories by constructing mental images in the minds of others.

☐ You may have been criticized because you like to talk a lot.

☐ Communication talents are valuable because your abilities in this area enable you to reach out and connect with people. Your storytelling ability builds images in the minds of others and makes you a powerful person as you connect and bond with people.

COMPETITION

Competition is rooted in comparison. When you look at the world, you are instinctively aware of other people's performance. Their performance is the ultimate yardstick. No matter how hard you tried, no matter how worthy your intentions, if you reached your goal but did not outperform your peers, the achievement feels hollow. Like all competitors, you need other people. You need to compare. If you can compare, you can compete, and if you can compete, you can win. And when you win, there is no feeling quite like it. You like measurement because it facilitates comparisons. You like other competitors because they invigorate you. You like contests because they must produce a winner. You particularly like contests where you know you have the inside track to be the winner. Although you are gracious to your fellow competitors and even stoic in defeat, you don't compete for the fun of competing. You compete to win. Over time you will come to avoid contests where winning seems unlikely.

Scriptures that relate to the Competition theme:

Little children, you are from God, and have conquered them; for the one who is in you is greater than the one who is in the world.
1 John 4:4

Do you not know that in a race the runners all compete, but only one receives the prize? Run in such a way that you may win it. Athletes exercise self-control in all things; they do it to receive a perishable wreath, but we an imperishable one. So I do not run aimlessly.
1 Corinthians 9:24-26a

34

And there came out from the camp of the Philistines a champion named Goliath, of Gath, whose height was six cubits and a span. He had a helmet of bronze on his head, and he was armed with a coat of mail; the weight of the coat was five thousand shekels of bronze. He had greaves of bronze on his legs and a javelin of bronze slung between his shoulders. The shaft of his spear was like a weaver's beam, and his spear's head weighed six hundred shekels of iron; and his shield-bearer went before him. He stood and shouted to the ranks of Israel, "Why have you come out to draw up for battle? Am I not a Philistine, and are you not servants of Saul? Choose a man for yourselves, and let him come down to me. If he is able to fight with me and kill me, then we will be your servants; but if I prevail against him and kill him, then you shall be our servants and serve us." And the Philistine said, "Today I defy the ranks of Israel! Give me a man, that we may fight together."

1 Samuel 17:4-10

When this perishable body puts on imperishability, and this mortal body puts on immortality, then the saying that is written will be fulfilled:
"Death has been swallowed up in victory."
    "Where, O death, is your victory?
    Where, O death, is your sting?"
The sting of death is sin, and the power of sin is the law. But thanks be to God, who gives us the victory through our Lord Jesus Christ.

1 Corinthians 15:54-57

For further understanding of your talents, examine these five insights and select those that describe you best.

☐ You want to win, which usually means outperforming others.

☐ You will work very hard to excel past others.

☐ You constantly compare yourself and your performance to other people and their performances.

☐ You may not be willing to try something if you think you can't win. Other people may consider your competitiveness inappropriate and therefore push you away, reject you, or accuse you of being arrogant.

☐ Competition talents are valuable because through them you will influence and even push people in your group to achieve more than other groups. You bring energy to a group and can energize others to move to higher levels of excellence.

CONNECTEDNESS

Things happen for a reason. You are sure of it. You are sure of it because in your soul you know that we are all connected. Yes, we are individuals, responsible for our own judgments and in possession of our own free will, but nonetheless we are part of something larger. Some may call it the collective unconscious. Others may label it spirit or life force. But whatever your word of choice, you gain confidence from knowing that we are not isolated from one another or from the earth and the life on it. This feeling of Connectedness implies certain responsibilities. If we are all part of a larger picture, then we must not harm others because we will be harming ourselves. We must not exploit because we will be exploiting ourselves. Your awareness of these responsibilities creates your value system. You are considerate, caring, and accepting. Certain of the unity of humankind, you are a bridge builder for people of different cultures. Sensitive to the invisible hand, you can give others comfort that there is a purpose beyond our humdrum lives. The exact articles of your faith will depend on your upbringing and your culture, but your faith is strong. It sustains you and your close friends in the face of life's mysteries.

Scriptures that relate to the Connectedness theme:

We know that all things work together for good for those who love God, who are called according to his purpose.
Romans 8:28

Ask, and it will be given you; search, and you will find; knock, and the door will be opened for you. For everyone who asks receives, and everyone who searches finds, and for everyone who knocks, the door will be opened.

Matthew 7:7-8

But as it is, God arranged the members in the body, each one of them, as he chose. If all were a single member, where would the body be? As it is, there are many members, yet one body. The eye cannot say to the hand, "I have no need of you," nor again the head to the feet, "I have no need of you." . . . If one member suffers, all suffer together with it; if one member is honored, all rejoice together with it. Now you are the body of Christ and individually members of it.

1 Corinthians 12:18-21, 26-27

[Make] every effort to maintain the unity of the Spirit in the bond of peace. There is one body and one Spirit, just as you were called to the one hope of your calling, one Lord, one faith, one baptism, one God and Father of all, who is above all and through all and in all.

Ephesians 4:3-6

For further understanding of your talents, examine these five insights and select those that describe you best.

- ☐ You see that all things happen for a reason. All things are working together in a purposeful manner.

- ☐ You feel connected to life itself. Therefore, you feel a responsibility to be considerate, caring, and accepting toward others.

- ☐ You are a bridge builder for people from all backgrounds to come together and develop a faith that goes beyond themselves.

☐ When people and the world seem fractured, broken, and isolated, you become discouraged and sometimes distressed. For this reason, some may perceive you as too naïve or fragile.

☐ Connectedness talents are valuable because they provide you with conviction and faith that sustain and encourage you and your friends in difficult times. You believe that there's a plan, a design, and a power beyond the visible world that provide meaning, comfort, and confidence. Your Connectedness gives you hope and helps you to achieve your ultimate goals.

CONSISTENCY

Balance is important to you. You are keenly aware of the need to treat people the same, no matter what their station in life, so you do not want to see the scales tipped too far in any one person's favor. In your view this leads to selfishness and individualism. It leads to a world where some people gain an unfair advantage because of their connections or their background or their greasing of the wheels. This is truly offensive to you. You see yourself as a guardian against it. In direct contrast to this world of special favors, you believe that people function best in a consistent environment where the rules are clear and are applied to everyone equally. This is an environment where people know what is expected. It is predictable and evenhanded. It is fair. Here each person has an even chance to show his or her worth.

Scriptures that relate to the Consistency theme:

My brothers and sisters, do you with your acts of favoritism really believe in our glorious Lord Jesus Christ? . . . You do well if you really fulfill the royal law according to the scripture, "You shall love your neighbor as yourself." But if you show partiality, you commit sin and are convicted by the law as transgressors.
James 2:1, 8-9

For he makes his sun rise on the evil and on the good, and sends rain on the righteous and on the unrighteous.
Matthew 5:45

For by the grace given me I say to everyone among you not to think of yourself more highly than you ought to think, but to think with sober judgment, each according to the measure of faith that God has assigned.

Romans 12:3

For further understanding of your talents, examine these five insights and select those that describe you best.

- ☐ You try to treat everyone consistently by having clear rules and applying them to everyone in the same way.
- ☐ You are offended when some people gain an advantage because of their connections or the games they play.
- ☐ You believe that people work best in a consistent environment where the rules apply to everyone equally, and you work to create this type of environment.
- ☐ While you may see yourself as a guardian of what is right and a warrior against special treatment, some people may reject you for assuming that responsibility.
- ☐ Consistency talents are valuable because you can more easily recognize inconsistencies, and you can readily suggest changes that can create a more equitable world.

CONTEXT

You look back. You look back because that is where the answers lie. You look back to understand the present. From your vantage point the present is unstable, a confusing clamor of competing voices. It is only by casting your mind back to an earlier time, a time when the plans were being drawn up, that the present regains its stability. The earlier time was a simpler time. It was a time of blueprints. As you look back, you begin to see these blueprints emerge. You realize what the initial intentions were. These blueprints or intentions have since become so embellished that they are almost unrecognizable, but now this Context theme reveals them again. This understanding brings you confidence. No longer disoriented, you make better decisions because you sense the underlying structure. You become a better partner because you understand how your colleagues came to be who they are. And counterintuitively you become wiser about the future because you saw its seeds being sown in the past. Faced with new people and new situations, it will take you a little time to orient yourself, but you must give yourself this time. You must discipline yourself to ask the questions and allow the blueprints to emerge because no matter what the situation, if you haven't seen the blueprints, you will have less confidence in your decisions.

Scriptures that relate to the Context theme:

But take care and watch yourselves closely, so as neither to forget the things that your eyes have seen nor to let them slip from your mind all the days of your life; make them known to your children and your children's children — how you once stood before the LORD your God at Horeb, when the LORD said to me, "Assemble the people for me, and I will let them hear my words, so that they may learn to fear me as long as they live on the earth, and may teach their children so";
Deuteronomy 4:9-10

Long ago God spoke to our ancestors in many and various ways by the prophets, but in these last days he has spoken to us by a Son, whom he appointed heir of all things, through whom he also created the worlds.
Hebrews 1:1-2

Joshua said to them, "Pass on before the ark of the LORD your God into the middle of the Jordan, and each of you take up a stone on his shoulder, one for each of the tribes of the Israelites, so that this may be a sign among you. When your children ask in time to come, 'What do those stones mean to you?' then you shall tell them that the waters of the Jordan were cut off in front of the ark of the covenant of the LORD. When it crossed over the Jordan, the waters of the Jordan were cut off. So these stones shall be to the Israelites a memorial forever."
Joshua 4:5-7

That which is, already has been; that which is to be, already is; and God seeks out what has gone by.
Ecclesiastes 3:15

"Do not think that I have come to abolish the law or the prophets; I have come not to abolish but to fulfill."
Matthew 5:17

For further understanding of your talents, examine these five insights and select those that describe you best.

☐ You look to the past to understand the present.

☐ You see patterns that emerge from studying what happened before.

☐ You learn best when you place what is to be learned into the context of other important dynamics and the history of what you are learning.

☐ You may feel disoriented when you can't see patterns stemming from the past. Others may become impatient with you as you strive to build an understanding of life's many complexities. You may be perceived as "slow" because you want to understand how we got to where we are.

☐ Context talents are valuable because they provide perspective that enhances your ability and confidence in making decisions and action planning.

DELIBERATIVE

You are careful. You are vigilant. You are a private person. You know that the world is an unpredictable place. Everything may seem in order, but beneath the surface you sense the many risks. Rather than denying these risks, you draw each one out into the open. Then each risk can be identified, assessed, and ultimately reduced. Thus, you are a fairly serious person who approaches life with a certain reserve. For example, you like to plan ahead so as to anticipate what might go wrong. You select your friends cautiously and keep your own counsel when the conversation turns to personal matters. You are careful not to give too much praise and recognition, lest it be misconstrued. If some people don't like you because you are not as effusive as others, then so be it. For you, life is not a popularity contest. Life is something of a minefield. Others can run through it recklessly if they so choose, but you take a different approach. You identify the dangers, weigh their relative impact, and then place your feet deliberately. You walk with care.

Scriptures that relate to the Deliberative theme:

Be careful then how you live, not as unwise people but as wise, making the most of the time, because the days are evil.
Ephesians 5:15-16

You must understand this, my beloved: let everyone be quick to listen, slow to speak, slow to anger; for your anger does not produce God's righteousness.
James 1:19-20

For which of you, intending to build a tower, does not first sit down and estimate the cost, to see whether he has enough to complete it? Otherwise, when he has laid a foundation and is not able to finish, all who see it will begin to ridicule him, saying, "This fellow began to build and was not able to finish."
Luke 14:28-30

For further understanding of your talents, examine these five insights and select those that describe you best.

☐ You take great care as you consider options, thinking through the pros and cons of each alternative.

☐ To you, making the correct decision is more important than the time it takes to do so.

☐ You make very good decisions. In fact, you would change few of your choices or decisions.

☐ You may exhaust yourself and others as you make your decisions cautiously and slowly. You always think about the risks and what might go wrong. Therefore, some may falsely judge you as a pessimist. You may even be falsely categorized as less intelligent when in fact you are doing some very deep thinking.

☐ Deliberative talents are valuable because they enable you to eliminate or reduce errors by thoroughly considering each option. Though this may add time to the decision-making process, the results are usually worth the wait.

DEVELOPER

You see the potential in others. Very often, in fact, potential is all you see. In your view no individual is fully formed. On the contrary, each individual is a work in progress, alive with possibilities. And you are drawn toward people for this very reason. When you interact with others, your goal is to help them experience success. You look for ways to challenge them. You devise interesting experiences that can stretch them and help them grow. And all the while you are on the lookout for the signs of growth — a new behavior learned or modified, a slight improvement in a skill, a glimpse of excellence or of "flow" where previously there were only halting steps. For you these small increments — invisible to some — are clear signs of potential being realized. These signs of growth in others are your fuel. They bring you strength and satisfaction. Over time many will seek you out for help and encouragement because on some level they know that your helpfulness is both genuine and fulfilling to you.

Scriptures that relate to the Developer theme:

News of this came to the ears of the church in Jerusalem, and they sent Barnabas to Antioch. When he came and saw the grace of God, he rejoiced, and he exhorted them all to remain faithful to the Lord with steadfast devotion; for he was a good man, full of the Holy Spirit and of faith. And a great many people were brought to the Lord. Then Barnabas went to Tarsus to look for Saul, and when he had found him, he brought him to Antioch.

So it was that for an entire year they met with the church and taught a great many people, and it was in Antioch that the disciples were first called "Christians."

Acts 11:22-26

I thank my God every time I remember you, constantly praying with joy in every one of my prayers for all of you, because of your sharing in the gospel from the first day until now. I am confident of this, that the one who began a good work among you will bring it to completion by the day of Jesus Christ.

Philippians 1:3-6

But we were gentle among you, like a nurse tenderly caring for her own children. So deeply do we care for you that we are determined to share with you not only the gospel of God but also our own selves, because you have become very dear to us . . . As you know, we dealt with each one of you like a father with his children, urging and encouraging you and pleading that you lead a life worthy of God, who calls you into his own kingdom and glory.

1 Thessalonians 2:7b-8, 11-12

and what you have heard from me through many witnesses entrust to faithful people who will be able to teach others as well.

2 Timothy 2:2

For further understanding of your talents, examine these five insights and select those that describe you best.

- ☐ You can see how other people can move, change, grow, and develop for the better.
- ☐ You love to see others make progress, and you will notice even the slightest progress.

☐ When you are a part of someone's development, it is the best experience in the world for you.

☐ Other people may not be as interested or ready to make the progress that you want them to make. Therefore, you may become frustrated when people don't want to improve, and you may feel frustrated or hurt when other people push you away because they feel pressured to improve.

☐ Developer talents are valuable because they help you see the potential in others and move them in that direction. People usually grow and improve in the presence of a developer. When you fully apply your Developer talents, it is as if you are educating, counseling, and encouraging people all the time.

DISCIPLINE

Your world needs to be predictable. It needs to be ordered and planned. So you instinctively impose structure on your world. You set up routines. You focus on timelines and deadlines. You break long-term projects into a series of specific short-term plans, and you work through each plan diligently. You are not necessarily neat and clean, but you do need precision. Faced with the inherent messiness of life, you want to feel in control. The routines, the timelines, the structure, all of these help create this feeling of control. Lacking this theme of Discipline, others may sometimes resent your need for order, but there need not be conflict. You must understand that not everyone feels your urge for predictability; they have other ways of getting things done. Likewise, you can help them understand and even appreciate your need for structure. Your dislike of surprises, your impatience with errors, your routines, and your detail orientation don't need to be misinterpreted as controlling behaviors that box people in. Rather, these behaviors can be understood as your instinctive method for maintaining your progress and your productivity in the face of life's many distractions.

Scriptures that relate to the Discipline theme:

But all things should be done decently and in order.
1 Corinthians 14:40

*All this, in writing at the LORD's direction, he made clear to me —
the plan of all the works.*
1 Chronicles 28:19

*The plans of the diligent lead surely to abundance,
but everyone who is hasty comes only to want.*
Proverbs 21:5

For further understanding of your talents, examine these five insights and select those that describe you best.

☐ You find ways to organize yourself to get things done on time.

☐ You tend to place yourself in productive environments.

☐ You create order and structure where it is needed.

☐ Some people may label you as compulsive or a control freak because of your ability to discipline yourself and structure your world. But these attributes make you productive — usually more so than your critics.

☐ Discipline talents are valuable because they make you efficient *and* effective. First, they motivate you to organize tasks. Then, they keep you motivated to complete those tasks.

EMPATHY

You can sense the emotions of those around you. You can feel what they are feeling as though their feelings are your own. Intuitively, you are able to see the world through their eyes and share their perspective. You do not necessarily agree with each person's perspective. You do not necessarily feel pity for each person's predicament — this would be sympathy, not Empathy. You do not necessarily condone the choices each person makes, but you do understand. This instinctive ability to understand is powerful. You hear the unvoiced questions. You anticipate the need. Where others grapple for words, you seem to find the right words and the right tone. You help people find the right phrases to express their feelings — to themselves as well as to others. You help them give voice to their emotional life. For all these reasons other people are drawn to you.

Scriptures that relate to the Empathy theme:

When Jesus saw her weeping, and the Jews who came with her also weeping, he was greatly disturbed in spirit and deeply moved. He said, "Where have you laid him?" They said to him, "Lord, come and see." Jesus began to weep.
John 11:33-35

Rejoice with those who rejoice, weep with those who weep.
Romans 12:15

Now there was a woman who had been suffering from hemorrhages for twelve years; and though she had spent all she had

on physicians, no one could cure her. She came up behind him and touched the fringe of his clothes, and immediately her hemorrhage stopped. Then Jesus asked, "Who touched me?" When all denied it, Peter said, "Master, the crowds surround you and press in on you." But Jesus said, "Someone touched me; for I noticed that power had gone out from me." When the woman saw that she could not remain hidden, she came trembling; and falling down before him, she declared in the presence of all the people why she had touched him, and how she had been immediately healed. He said to her, "Daughter, your faith has made you well; go in peace."
Luke 8:43-48

For further understanding of your talents, examine these five insights and select those that describe you best.

☐ You can sense what it feels like to be someone else.

☐ You can pick up on the pain and joy of others — sometimes before they can express it. Other people feel heard by you and experience your compassion.

☐ Because you can quickly understand others, people are drawn to you when they have a need or a problem, especially in relationships.

☐ Your Empathy can be challenging because you may become overwhelmed with all of the emotions you can pick up in a day. Roles and relationships in which people project their negative emotions your way are hard on you. You can become exhausted from the emotions you pick up from others.

☐ Empathy talents are valuable because they enable you to form very close, supportive relationships in which you help and encourage others.

53

FOCUS

"Where am I headed?" you ask yourself. You ask this question every day. Guided by this theme of Focus, you need a clear destination. Lacking one, your life and your work can quickly become frustrating. And so each year, each month, and even each week you set goals. These goals then serve as your compass, helping you determine priorities and make the necessary corrections to get back on course. Your Focus is powerful because it forces you to filter; you instinctively evaluate whether or not a particular action will help you move toward your goal. Those that don't are ignored. In the end, then, your Focus forces you to be efficient. Naturally, the flip side of this is that it causes you to become impatient with delays, obstacles, and even tangents, no matter how intriguing they appear to be. This makes you an extremely valuable team member. When others start to wander down other avenues, you bring them back to the main road. Your Focus reminds everyone that if something is not helping you move toward your destination, then it is not important. And if it is not important, then it is not worth your time. You keep everyone on point.

Scriptures that relate to the Focus theme:

When the days drew near for him to be taken up, he set his face to go to Jerusalem.
Luke 9:51

Not that I have already obtained this or have already reached the goal; but I press on to make it my own, because Christ Jesus has made me his own. Beloved, I do not consider that I have made it my own; but this one thing I do: forgetting what lies behind and straining forward to what lies ahead, I press on toward the goal for the prize of the heavenly call of God in Christ Jesus.

Philippians 3:12-14

Therefore, since we are surrounded by so great a cloud of witnesses, let us also lay aside every weight and the sin that clings so closely, and let us run with perseverance the race that is set before us, looking to Jesus the pioneer and perfecter of our faith, who for the sake of the joy that was set before him endured the cross, disregarding its shame, and has taken his seat at the right hand of the throne of God.

Hebrews 12:1-2

For further understanding of your talents, examine these five insights and select those that describe you best.

☐ You can take a direction, follow through, and make the necessary corrections to stay on track.

☐ You prioritize your life and tasks, and then you take action.

☐ You set goals that keep you effective and efficient.

☐ You become frustrated when you can't determine what a group is trying to do. Likewise, your life and work become frustrating when your goals are unclear.

☐ Focus talents are valuable because you can quickly evaluate, determine priorities, and get yourself and groups on course quickly. Your Focus motivates you to be efficient. You get a lot done because you don't get easily distracted.

FUTURISTIC

"Wouldn't it be great if . . ." You are the kind of person who loves to peer over the horizon. The future fascinates you. As if it were projected on the wall, you see in detail what the future might hold, and this detailed picture keeps pulling you forward, into tomorrow. While the exact content of the picture will depend on your other strengths and interests — a better product, a better team, a better life, or a better world — it will always be inspirational to you. You are a dreamer who sees visions of what could be and who cherishes those visions. When the present proves too frustrating and the people around you too pragmatic, you conjure up your visions of the future and they energize you. They can energize others, too. In fact, very often people look to you to describe your visions of the future. They want a picture that can raise their sights and thereby their spirits. You can paint it for them. Practice. Choose your words carefully. Make the picture as vivid as possible. People will want to latch on to the hope you bring.

Scriptures that relate to the Futuristic theme:

Where there is no vision, the people perish.
Proverbs 29:18a (King James Version)

Then afterward
I will pour out my spirit on all flesh;
your sons and your daughters shall prophesy,
your old men shall dream dreams,
your young men shall see visions.
Joel 2:28

Once Joseph had a dream, and when he told it to his brothers, they hated him even more. He said to them, "Listen to this dream that I dreamed. There we were, binding sheaves in the field. Suddenly my sheaf rose and stood upright; then your sheaves gathered around it, and bowed down to my sheaf." His brothers said to him, "Are you indeed to reign over us? Are you indeed to have dominion over us?" So they hated him even more because of his dreams and his words.

Genesis 37:5-8

I consider that the sufferings of this present time are not worth comparing with the glory about to be revealed to us. For the creation waits with eager longing for the revealing of the children of God; for the creation was subjected to futility, not of its own will but by the will of the one who subjected it, in hope that the creation itself will be set free from its bondage to decay and will obtain the freedom of the glory of the children of God.

Romans 8:18-21

For surely I know the plans I have for you, says the LORD, plans for your welfare and not for harm, to give you a future with hope.

Jeremiah 29:11

For further understanding of your talents, examine these five insights and select those that describe you best.

☐ You are fascinated by the future, and you usually see the future positively.

☐ You can see in detail what the future might hold.

☐ You can energize yourself and others by your vision of what could be. You can clearly see possibilities.

☐ Others may dismiss you as a dreamer. You may become frustrated by present circumstances and discouraged by highly pragmatic people who can't or won't see the possibilities in the future that are so clear to you.

☐ Futuristic talents are valuable because your vision raises others' sights and focuses their energies.

HARMONY

You look for areas of agreement. In your view there is little to be gained from conflict and friction, so you seek to hold them to a minimum. When you know that the people around you hold differing views, you try to find the common ground. You try to steer them away from confrontation and toward harmony. In fact, harmony is one of your guiding values. You can't quite believe how much time is wasted by people trying to impose their views on others. Wouldn't we all be more productive if we kept our opinions in check and instead looked for consensus and support? You believe we would, and you live by that belief. When others are sounding off about their goals, their claims, and their fervently held opinions, you hold your peace. When others strike out in a direction, you will willingly, in the service of harmony, modify your own objectives to merge with theirs (as long as their basic values do not clash with yours). When others start to argue about their pet theory or concept, you steer clear of the debate, preferring to talk about practical, down-to-earth matters on which you can all agree. In your view we are all in the same boat, and we need this boat to get where we are going. It is a good boat. There is no need to rock it just to show that you can.

Scriptures that relate to the Harmony theme:

Live in harmony with one another.

Romans 12:16a

Blessed are the peacemakers, for they will be called children of God.

Matthew 5:9

Now I appeal to you, brothers and sisters, by the name of our Lord Jesus Christ, that all of you be in agreement and that there be no divisions among you, but that you be united in the same mind and the same purpose.
1 Corinthians 1:10

*How very good and pleasant it is
when kindred live together in unity!*
Psalms 133:1

Starting a quarrel is like breaching a dam; so drop the matter before a dispute breaks out.
Proverbs 17:14 (NIV)

For further understanding of your talents, examine these five insights and select those that describe you best.

☐ You want peace, and you try to bring people together.

☐ You can see points that people have in common, even when they are in conflict.

☐ You seek to help individuals, families, and organizations work together.

☐ Some people may criticize you or misunderstand you. They may say that you lack courage. You too may see your desire for harmony as only an avoidance of conflict.

☐ Harmony talents are valuable because you see what people have in common and try to help them to interact on the basis of shared points of view. This binds people to you and helps groups come together. Groups, organizations, and teams function better and achieve more because of what you do to bring people together.

IDEATION

You are fascinated by ideas. What is an idea? An idea is a concept, the best explanation of the most events. You are delighted when you discover beneath the complex surface an elegantly simple concept to explain why things are the way they are. An idea is a connection. Yours is the kind of mind that is always looking for connections, and so you are intrigued when seemingly disparate phenomena can be linked by an obscure connection. An idea is a new perspective on familiar challenges. You revel in taking the world we all know and turning it around so we can view it from a strange but strangely enlightening angle. You love all these ideas because they are profound, because they are novel, because they are clarifying, because they are contrary, because they are bizarre. For all these reasons you derive a jolt of energy whenever a new idea occurs to you. Others may label you creative or original or conceptual or even smart. Perhaps you are all of these. Who can be sure? What you are sure of is that ideas are thrilling. And on most days this is enough.

Scriptures that relate to the Ideation theme:

For I am about to create new heavens
and a new earth;
the former things shall not be remembered
or come to mind.
But be glad and rejoice forever

in what I am creating;
for I am about to create Jerusalem as a joy,
    and its people as a delight.
Isaiah 65:17-18

Do not be conformed to this world, but be transformed by the
renewing of your minds, so that you may discern what is the
will of God — what is good and acceptable and perfect.
Romans 12:2

"You are worthy, our Lord and God,
    to receive glory and honor and power,
for you created all things,
    and by your will they existed and were created."
Revelation 4:11

For further understanding of your talents, examine these five insights and select those that describe you best.

☐ You are a creative person, and you appreciate originality.

☐ You like free-thinking experiences such as brainstorming and discussion groups.

☐ You love new ideas and concepts.

☐ At times, it may seem like you get lost in the world of ideas, and others may think you are a little "spacey."

☐ Ideation talents are valuable because they enable you to look for new connections and generate new insights when things don't make sense. You are able to help others take the world they know and turn it around so that they can see it from a new point of view.

INCLUDER

"Stretch the circle wider." This is the philosophy around which you orient your life. You want to include people and make them feel part of the group. In direct contrast to those who are drawn only to exclusive groups, you actively avoid those groups that exclude others. You want to expand the group so that as many people as possible can benefit from its support. You hate the sight of someone on the outside looking in. You want to draw them in so that they can feel the warmth of the group. You are an instinctively accepting person. Regardless of race or sex or nationality or personality or faith, you cast few judgments. Judgments can hurt a person's feelings. Why do that if you don't have to? Your accepting nature does not necessarily rest on a belief that each of us is different and that one should respect these differences. Rather, it rests on your conviction that fundamentally we are all the same. We are all equally important. Thus, no one should be ignored. Each of us should be included. It is the least we all deserve.

Scriptures that relate to the Includer theme:

There is no longer Jew or Greek, there is no longer slave or free, there is no longer male and female; for all of you are one in Christ Jesus.
Galatians 3:28

For God so loved the world that he gave his only Son, so that everyone who believes in him may not perish but may have eternal life.
John 3:16

So if you consider me your partner, welcome him as you would welcome me.

Philemon 17

Welcome one another, therefore, just as Christ has welcomed you, for the glory of God.

Romans 15:7

For further understanding of your talents, examine these five insights and select those that describe you best.

☐ You notice people who feel like outsiders or who feel unappreciated.

☐ You are not content when people are left out, so you try to reach out to the "outsiders," and you try to bring them in.

☐ People see you as accepting and sense that you want them to be included.

☐ In your attempts to include others, you may be rejected by the very people you try to include. You may have to confront your own fears as you seek to include those who may reject you. You may also have to deal with people who misunderstand your actions and yet do nothing to reach out to those who feel left out.

☐ Includer talents are valuable because they enable you to help individuals, groups, organizations, and communities to be unified and effective. People who have felt rejected will appreciate your efforts.

INDIVIDUALIZATION

Your Individualization theme leads you to be intrigued by the unique qualities of each person. You are impatient with generalizations or "types" because you don't want to obscure what is special and distinct about each person. Instead, you focus on the differences between individuals. You instinctively observe each person's style, each person's motivation, how each thinks, and how each builds relationships. You hear the one-of-a-kind stories in each person's life. This theme explains why you pick your friends just the right birthday gift, why you know that one person prefers praise in public and another detests it, and why you tailor your teaching style to accommodate one person's need to be shown and another's desire to "figure it out as I go." Because you are such a keen observer of other people's strengths, you can draw out the best in each person. This Individualization theme also helps you build productive teams. While some search around for the perfect team "structure" or "process," you know instinctively that the secret to great teams is casting by individual strengths so that everyone can do a lot of what they do well.

Scriptures that relate to the Individualization theme:

But even the hairs of your head are all counted. Do not be afraid; you are of more value than many sparrows.
Luke 12:7

O LORD, you have searched me and known me.
You know when I sit down and when I rise up;
    you discern my thoughts from far away.
You search out my path and my lying down,
    and are acquainted with all my ways.
Psalm 139:1-3

But the LORD said to Samuel, "Do not look on his appearance
or on the height of his stature, because I have rejected him; for
the LORD does not see as mortals see; they look on the outward
appearance, but the LORD looks on the heart."
1 Samuel 16:7

Then Jesus summoned his twelve disciples and gave them
authority over unclean spirits, to cast them out, and to cure
every disease and every sickness. These are the names of the
twelve apostles: first, Simon, also known as Peter, and his brother
Andrew; James son of Zebedee, and his brother John; Philip
and Bartholomew; Thomas and Matthew the tax collector; James
son of Alphaeus, and Thaddaeus; Simon the Cananaean, and
Judas Iscariot, the one who betrayed him.
Matthew 10:1-4

For further understanding of your talents, examine these five insights and select those that describe you best.

- ☐ You see each person as a distinct, one-of-a-kind individual.
- ☐ You can see how people who are very different can work together.
- ☐ You can build productive teams of people because you can see the talents of people and then structure groups around those talents.

☐ Because you see individuals so distinctly and try to relate to them in terms of their specific characteristics, relating to people can be taxing and even overwhelming.

☐ Individualization talents are valuable because they help you form powerful relationships with people. Those people know that you take them seriously and that you see them as distinct individuals. For many, this is very valuable, as it brings trust and intensity to your relationships.

INPUT

You are inquisitive. You collect things. You might collect information — words, facts, books, and quotations — or you might collect tangible objects such as butterflies, baseball cards, porcelain dolls, or sepia photographs. Whatever you collect, you collect it because it interests you. And yours is the kind of mind that finds so many things interesting. The world is exciting precisely because of its infinite variety and complexity. If you read a great deal, it is not necessarily to refine your theories but, rather, to add more information to your archives. If you like to travel, it is because each new location offers novel artifacts and facts. These can be acquired and then stored away. Why are they worth storing? At the time of storing it is often hard to say exactly when or why you might need them, but who knows when they might become useful? With all those possible uses in mind, you really don't feel comfortable throwing anything away. So you keep acquiring and compiling and filing stuff away. It's interesting. It keeps your mind fresh. And perhaps one day some of it will prove valuable.

Scriptures that relate to the Input theme:

But there are also many other things that Jesus did; if every one of them were written down, I suppose that the world itself could not contain the books that would be written.
John 21:25

When you come, bring the cloak that I left with Carpus at Troas, also the books, and above all the parchments.
2 Timothy 4:13

My child, if you accept my words
    and treasure up my commandments within you,
making your ear attentive to wisdom
    and inclining your heart to understanding;
if you indeed cry out for insight,
    and raise your voice for understanding;
if you seek it like silver,
    and search for it as for hidden treasures —
then you will understand the fear of the LORD
    and find the knowledge of God.

Proverbs 2:1-5

For further understanding of your talents, examine these five insights and select those that describe you best.

- ☐ You always want to know more. You crave information.
- ☐ You like to collect certain things, such as ideas, books, memorabilia, quotations, and facts.
- ☐ You have an active curiosity. You find many things very interesting.
- ☐ You may have difficulty getting started or completing a project because you feel like you never have enough information. Going to a library or "surfing the Net" may turn into hours once your curiosity takes off, and you may have difficulties filing and housing all of the information and ideas you acquire.
- ☐ Input talents are valuable because they keep your mind active and lead you to become knowledgeable. You are likely to become an expert in one or more areas.

INTELLECTION

You like to think. You like mental activity. You like exercising the "muscles" of your brain, stretching them in multiple directions. This need for mental activity may be focused; for example, you may be trying to solve a problem or develop an idea or understand another person's feelings. The exact focus will depend on your other strengths. On the other hand, this mental activity may very well lack focus. The theme of Intellection does not dictate what you are thinking about; it simply describes that you like to think. You are the kind of person who enjoys your time alone because it is your time for musing and reflection. You are introspective. In a sense you are your own best companion, as you pose yourself questions and try out answers on yourself to see how they sound. This introspection may lead you to a slight sense of discontent as you compare what you are actually doing with all the thoughts and ideas that your mind conceives. Or this introspection may tend toward more pragmatic matters such as the events of the day or a conversation that you plan to have later. Wherever it leads you, this mental hum is one of the constants of your life.

Scriptures that relate to the Intellection theme:

After three days they found him in the temple, sitting among the teachers, listening to them and asking them questions. And all who heard him were amazed at his understanding and his answers.
Luke 2:46-47

So he argued in the synagogue with the Jews and the devout persons, and also in the marketplace every day with those who happened to be there. Also some Epicurean and Stoic philosophers debated with him. Some said, "What does this babbler want to say?" Others said, "He seems to be a proclaimer of foreign divinities." (This was because he was telling the good news about Jesus and the resurrection.)

Acts 17:17-18

He said to him, "You shall love the Lord your God with all your heart, and with all your soul, and with all your mind."

Matthew 22:37

Therefore prepare your minds for action; discipline yourselves; set all your hope on the grace that Jesus Christ will bring you when he is revealed.

1 Peter 1:13

For further understanding of your talents, examine these five insights and select those that describe you best.

☐ You love to study, and you prefer intellectual discussions.

☐ You like to think and to let your thoughts go in many directions.

☐ You like to spend time alone so you can reflect and ponder.

☐ You may become discouraged because there are so many things that you need to think about so carefully and thoroughly.

☐ Intellection talents are valuable because they help you find innovative ideas and solutions.

LEARNER

You love to learn. The subject matter that interests you most will be determined by your other themes and experiences, but whatever the subject, you will always be drawn to the process of learning. The process, more than the content or the result, is especially exciting for you. You are energized by the steady and deliberate journey from ignorance to competence. The thrill of the first few facts, the early efforts to recite or practice what you have learned, the growing confidence of a skill mastered — this is the process that entices you. Your excitement leads you to engage in adult learning experiences — yoga or piano lessons or graduate classes. It enables you to thrive in dynamic work environments where you are asked to take on short project assignments and are expected to learn a lot about the new subject matter in a short period of time and then move on to the next one. This Learner theme does not necessarily mean that you seek to become the subject matter expert, or that you are striving for the respect that accompanies a professional or academic credential. The outcome of the learning is less significant than the "getting there."

Scriptures that relate to the Learner theme:

Then the king commanded his palace master Ashpenaz to bring some of the Israelites of the royal family and of the nobility, young men without physical defect and handsome, versed in every branch of wisdom, endowed with knowledge and insight, and competent to serve in the king's palace; they were to be taught the literature and language of the Chaldeans.

Daniel 1:3-4

Now as they went on their way, he entered a certain village, where a woman named Martha welcomed him into her home. She had a sister named Mary, who sat at the Lord's feet and listened to what he was saying. But Martha was distracted by her many tasks; so she came to him and asked, "Lord, do you not care that my sister has left me to do all the work by myself? Tell her then to help me." But the Lord answered her, "Martha, Martha, you are worried and distracted by many things; there is need of only one thing. Mary has chosen the better part, which will not be taken away from her."

Luke 10:38-42

For Ezra had set his heart to study the law of the LORD, and to do it, and to teach the statutes and ordinances in Israel.

Ezra 7:10

But as for you, continue in what you have learned and firmly believed, knowing from whom you learned it, and how from childhood you have known the sacred writings that are able to instruct you for salvation through faith in Christ Jesus. All scripture is inspired by God and is useful for teaching, for reproof, for correction, and for training in righteousness, so that everyone who belongs to God may be proficient, equipped for every good work.

2 Timothy 3:14-17

For further understanding of your talents, examine these five insights and select those that describe you best.

☐ You want to continuously learn and improve.

☐ You enjoy the process of learning as much as what you actually learn.

☐ You get a thrill out of learning new facts, beginning a new subject, and mastering an important skill. Learning builds your confidence.

☐ You can get frustrated about wanting to learn so many different things because you fear you'll never be an expert.

☐ Learner talents are valuable because they propel you to thrive in a dynamic world where learning is a necessity. You can learn a lot in a short period of time.

MAXIMIZER

Excellence, not average, is your measure. Taking something from below average to slightly above average takes a great deal of effort and in your opinion is not very rewarding. Transforming something strong into something superb takes just as much effort but is much more thrilling. Strengths, whether yours or someone else's, fascinate you. Like a diver after pearls, you search them out, watching for the telltale signs of a strength. A glimpse of untutored excellence, rapid learning, a skill mastered without recourse to steps — all these are clues that a strength may be in play. And having found a strength, you feel compelled to nurture it, refine it, and stretch it toward excellence. You polish the pearl until it shines. This natural sorting of strengths means that others see you as discriminating. You choose to spend time with people who appreciate your particular strengths. Likewise, you are attracted to others who seem to have found and cultivated their own strengths. You tend to avoid those who want to fix you and make you well-rounded. You don't want to spend your life bemoaning what you lack. Rather, you want to capitalize on the gifts with which you are blessed. It's more fun. It's more productive. And, counterintuitively, it is more demanding.

Scriptures that relate to the Maximizer theme:

Now as you excel in everything — in faith, in speech, in knowledge, in utmost eagerness, and in our love for you — so we want you to excel also in this generous undertaking.
2 Corinthians 8:7

Out of all the gifts to you, you shall set apart every offering due to the LORD; the best of all of them is the part to be consecrated.

Numbers 18:29

But those who hope in the LORD will renew their strength. They will soar on wings like eagles; they will run and not grow weary, they will walk and not be faint.

Isaiah 40:31 (NIV)

After a long time the master of those slaves came and settled accounts with them. Then the one who had received the five talents came forward, bringing five more talents, saying, "Master, you handed over to me five talents; see, I have made five more talents." His master said to him, "Well done, good and trustworthy slave; you have been trustworthy in a few things, I will put you in charge of many things; enter into the joy of your master."

Matthew 25:19-21

For this reason I remind you to rekindle the gift of God that is within you through the laying on of my hands.

2 Timothy 1:6

For further understanding of your talents, examine these five insights and select those that describe you best.

☐ You see talents and strengths in others, sometimes before they do.

☐ You love to help others become excited by the potential of their natural talents.

☐ You have the capacity to see what people will do best and which jobs they will be good at. You can see how people's talents match the tasks that must be completed.

☐ Some people will be intimidated by your perceptiveness and drive for excellence. These people may want to keep you at a distance, and you may feel rejected or like there is something wrong with you.

☐ Maximizer talents are valuable because they help you focus on talents to stimulate personal and group excellence. If a group or organization is on the move toward excellence, a talented Maximizer is probably somewhere in the midst.

POSITIVITY

You are generous with praise, quick to smile, and always on the lookout for the positive in the situation. Some call you lighthearted. Others just wish that their glass were as full as yours seems to be. But either way, people want to be around you. Their world looks better around you because your enthusiasm is contagious. Lacking your energy and optimism, some find their world drab with repetition or, worse, heavy with pressure. You seem to find a way to lighten their spirit. You inject drama into every project. You celebrate every achievement. You find ways to make everything more exciting and more vital. Some cynics may reject your energy, but you are rarely dragged down. Your Positivity won't allow it. Somehow you can't quite escape your conviction that it is good to be alive, that work can be fun, and that no matter what the setbacks, one must never lose one's sense of humor.

Scriptures that relate to the Positivity theme:

A cheerful heart is a good medicine,
but a downcast spirit dries up the bones.
Proverbs 17:22

Finally, beloved, whatever is true, whatever is honorable, whatever is just, whatever is pure, whatever is pleasing, whatever is commendable, if there is any excellence and if there is anything worthy of praise, think about these things.
Philippians 4:8

Rejoice always, pray without ceasing, give thanks in all circumstances; for this is the will of God in Christ Jesus for you.
1 Thessalonians 5:16-18

Then he said to them, "Go your way, eat the fat and drink sweet wine and send portions of them to those for whom nothing is prepared, for this day is holy to our LORD; and do not be grieved, for the joy of the LORD is your strength."
Nehemiah 8:10

"But we had to celebrate and rejoice, because this brother of yours was dead and has come to life; he was lost and has been found."
Luke 15:32

For further understanding of your talents, examine these five insights and select those that describe you best.

☐ You bring enthusiasm to people, groups, and organizations.

☐ You can stimulate people to be more productive and become more hopeful.

☐ You can get people excited about what they are doing, and therefore they become more productive.

☐ Some people will criticize you for being so optimistic. They may say you are naïve, and that may cause you to doubt yourself.

☐ Positivity talents are valuable because they have such a helpful influence on the attitudes, motivation, and productive behaviors of others. Groups and individuals are energized to move toward excellence.

RELATOR

Relator describes your attitude toward your relationships. In simple terms, the Relator theme pulls you toward people you already know. You do not necessarily shy away from meeting new people — in fact, you may have other themes that cause you to enjoy the thrill of turning strangers into friends — but you do derive a great deal of pleasure and strength from being around your close friends. You are comfortable with intimacy. Once the initial connection has been made, you deliberately encourage a deepening of the relationship. You want to understand their feelings, their goals, their fears, and their dreams; and you want them to understand yours. You know that this kind of closeness implies a certain amount of risk — you might be taken advantage of — but you are willing to accept that risk. For you a relationship has value only if it is genuine. And the only way to know that is to entrust yourself to the other person. The more you share with each other, the more you risk together. The more you risk together, the more each of you proves your caring is genuine. These are your steps toward real friendship, and you take them willingly.

Scriptures that relate to the Relator theme:

Some friends play at friendship
but a true friend sticks closer than one's nearest kin.
Proverbs 18:24

Two are better than one, because they have a good reward for
their toil. For if they fall, one will lift up the other; but woe to

80

one who is alone and falls and does not have another to help. Again, if two lie together, they keep warm; but how can one keep warm alone? And though one might prevail against another, two will withstand one. A threefold cord is not quickly broken.

Ecclesiastes 4:9-12

Saul spoke with his son Jonathan and with all his servants about killing David. But Saul's son Jonathan took great delight in David. Jonathan told David, "My father Saul is trying to kill you; therefore be on guard tomorrow morning; stay in a secret place and hide yourself. I will go out and stand beside my father in the field where you are, and I will speak to my father about you; if I learn anything I will tell you." . . . Thus Jonathan made a covenant with the house of David, saying, "May the LORD seek out the enemies of David." Jonathan made David swear again by his love for him; for he loved him as he loved his own life.

1 Samuel 19:1-3, 20:16-17

For further understanding of your talents, examine these five insights and select those that describe you best.

☐ You can form close relationships with people, and you enjoy doing so.

☐ You receive profound satisfaction from working hard with friends to accomplish an important goal.

☐ You know many people, and you can relate with all kinds of people. But you also have a very small group of friends with whom you have an incredibly deep relationship.

☐ Some people may feel threatened or uncomfortable because

they can't bring themselves to have the close, intense personal relationships that you thrive on.

☐ Relator talents are valuable to organizations, groups, and individuals because they foster interpersonal relationships that lead to productivity.

RESPONSIBILITY

Your Responsibility theme forces you to take psychological ownership for anything you commit to, and whether large or small, you feel emotionally bound to follow it through to completion. Your good name depends on it. If for some reason you cannot deliver, you automatically start to look for ways to make it up to the other person. Apologies are not enough. Excuses and ration-alizations are totally unacceptable. You will not quite be able to live with yourself until you have made restitution. This conscientiousness, this near obsession for doing things right, and your impeccable ethics combine to create your reputation: utterly dependable. When assigning new responsibilities, people will look to you first because they know things will get done. When people come to you for help — and they soon will — you must be selective. Your willingness to volunteer may sometimes lead you to take on more than you should.

Scriptures that relate to the Responsibility theme:

So the presidents and the satraps tried to find grounds for complaint against Daniel in connection with the kingdom. But they could find no grounds for complaint or any corruption, because he was faithful, and no negligence or corruption could be found in him.

Daniel 6:4

A good name is to be chosen rather than great riches,
  and favor is better than silver or gold.

Proverbs 22:1

Not everyone who says to me, "Lord, Lord," will enter the kingdom of heaven, but only the one who does the will of my Father in heaven.

Matthew 7:21

Then the king will say to those at his right hand, "Come, you that are blessed by my Father, inherit the kingdom prepared for you from the foundation of the world; for I was hungry and you gave me food, I was thirsty and you gave me something to drink, I was a stranger and you welcomed me, I was naked and you gave me clothing, I was sick and you took care of me, I was in prison and you visited me." Then the righteous will answer him, "Lord, when was it that we saw you hungry and gave you food, or thirsty and gave you something to drink? And when was it that we saw you a stranger and welcomed you, or naked and gave you clothing? And when was it that we saw you sick or in prison and visited you?" And the king will answer them, "Truly I tell you, just as you did it to one of the least of these who are members of my family, you did it to me."

Matthew 25:34-40

For further understanding of your talents, examine these five insights and select those that describe you best.

- ☐ You are dependable, and people know that they can count on you.

- ☐ You don't want to let people down, and you will work very hard to fulfill all your responsibilities and keep your word.

- ☐ You have many obligations and commitments because so many people know that they can count on you. Therefore, more and more people come to you.

☐ With the responsibility you feel to the people who come to you and with the demands that each of them brings, you often feel overwhelmed and under pressure to perform.

☐ Responsibility talents are valuable because they lead others to trust you and to become more responsible themselves. You might be more of a role model than you realize.

RESTORATIVE

You love to solve problems. Whereas some are dismayed when they encounter yet another breakdown, you can be energized by it. You enjoy the challenge of analyzing the symptoms, identifying what is wrong, and finding the solution. You may prefer practical problems or conceptual ones or personal ones. You may seek out specific kinds of problems that you have met many times before and that you are confident you can fix. Or you may feel the greatest push when faced with complex and unfamiliar problems. Your exact preferences are determined by your other themes and experiences. But what is certain is that you enjoy bringing things back to life. It is a wonderful feeling to identify the undermining factor(s), eradicate them, and restore something to its true glory. Intuitively, you know that without your intervention, this thing — this machine, this technique, this person, this company — might have ceased to function. You fixed it, resuscitated it, rekindled its vitality. Phrasing it the way you might, you saved it.

Scriptures that relate to the Restorative theme:

Then Levi gave a great banquet for him in his house; and there was a large crowd of tax collectors and others sitting at the table with them. The Pharisees and their scribes were complaining to his disciples, saying, "Why do you eat and drink with tax collectors and sinners?" Jesus answered, "Those who are well have no need of a physician, but those who are sick; I have come to call not the righteous but sinners to repentance."
Luke 5:29-32

My friends, if anyone is detected in a transgression, you who have received the Spirit should restore such a one in a spirit of gentleness. Take care that you yourselves are not tempted.
Galatians 6:1

The LORD is my shepherd, I shall not want.
He makes me lie down in green pastures; he leads me beside still waters; he restores my soul.
Psalm 23:1-3a

For further understanding of your talents, examine these five insights and select those that describe you best.

☐ You readily take on projects that others believe "can't be saved."

☐ You can analyze a situation and identify potential short-comings and what needs to be fixed.

☐ You quickly recognize problems that others may not detect.

☐ Other people may not like the fact that you can so quickly determine the problems and weaknesses in people, situations, and organizations. They may find this ability embarrassing, even if your assessments and solutions are accurate.

☐ Restorative talents are valuable because through them you are energized, rather than defeated, by problems.

SELF-ASSURANCE

Self-Assurance is similar to self-confidence. In the deepest part of you, you have faith in your strengths. You know that you are able — able to take risks, able to meet new challenges, able to stake claims, and, most important, able to deliver. But Self-Assurance is more than just self-confidence. Blessed with the theme of Self-Assurance, you have confidence not only in your abilities but in your judgment. When you look at the world, you know that your perspective is unique and distinct. And because no one sees exactly what you see, you know that no one can make your decisions for you. No one can tell you what to think. They can guide. They can suggest. But you alone have the authority to form conclusions, make decisions, and act. This authority, this final accountability for the living of your life, does not intimidate you. On the contrary, it feels natural to you. No matter what the situation, you seem to know what the right decision is. This theme lends you an aura of certainty. Unlike many, you are not easily swayed by someone else's arguments, no matter how persuasive they may be. This Self-Assurance may be quiet or loud, depending on your other themes, but it is solid. It is strong. Like the keel of a ship, it withstands many different pressures and keeps you on your course.

Scriptures that relate to the Self-Assurance theme:

Now faith is the assurance of things hoped for, the conviction of things not seen.
Hebrews 11:1

But I am not ashamed, for I know the one in whom I have put my trust, and I am sure that he is able to guard until that day what I have entrusted to him.

2 Timothy 1:12b

He had another dream, and told it to his brothers, saying, "Look, I have had another dream: the sun, the moon, and eleven stars were bowing down to me." But when he told it to his father and to his brothers, his father rebuked him, and said to him, "What kind of dream is this that you have had? Shall we indeed come, I and your mother and your brothers, and bow to the ground before you?" So his brothers were jealous of him, but his father kept the matter in mind.

Genesis 37:9-11

For further understanding of your talents, examine these five insights and select those that describe you best.

☐ You are confident about your ability to manage your life.

☐ You can "bounce back" from disappointments and crises.

☐ You believe that your decisions are right and that your perspective is unique and distinct.

☐ Other people may see your self-assurance as a type of pride or arrogance. Some people may criticize you when they wish that they had your confidence. Sometimes people want to get close to you because they hope that some of your confidence will rub off on them. But other people will keep you away because they don't have your confidence and are afraid that you will see through them.

89

☐ Self-Assurance talents are valuable because they keep you strong as you withstand many pressures, as you stay on your course, and as you willingly claim the authority to form conclusions, make decisions, and act.

SIGNIFICANCE

You want to be very significant in the eyes of other people. In the truest sense of the word you want to be recognized. You want to be heard. You want to stand out. You want to be known. In particular, you want to be known and appreciated for the unique strengths you bring. You feel a need to be admired as credible, professional, and successful. Likewise, you want to associate with others who are credible, professional, and successful. And if they aren't, you will push them to achieve until they are. Or you will move on. An independent spirit, you want your work to be a way of life rather than a job, and in that work you want to be given free rein, the leeway to do things your way. Your yearnings feel intense to you, and you honor those yearnings. And so your life is filled with goals, achievements, or qualifications that you crave. Whatever your focus — and each person is distinct — your Significance theme will keep pulling you upward, away from the mediocre toward the exceptional. It is the theme that keeps you reaching.

Scriptures that relate to the Significance theme:

You are the light of the world. A city built on a hill cannot be hid. No one after lighting a lamp puts it under the bushel basket, but on the lampstand, and it gives light to all in the house. In the same way, let your light shine before others, so that they may see your good works and give glory to your Father in heaven.

Matthew 5:14-16

I came that they may have life, and have it abundantly.
John 10:10b

For though you might have ten thousand guardians in Christ, you do not have many fathers. Indeed, in Christ Jesus I became your father through the gospel. I appeal to you, then, be imitators of me.

1 Corinthians 4:15-16

For further understanding of your talents, examine these five insights and select those that describe you best.

☐ You probably enjoy receiving public recognition for the differences you make.

☐ You want to have an impact on other people, groups, and society as a whole.

☐ You want the contributions you make to be viewed as substantial, powerful, and significant.

☐ Although many people will appreciate your talent in this theme, others may be intimidated by it, and they might not say so. Instead, they may say that you are "just wanting attention" or that you are egocentric.

☐ Significance talents are valuable because they can be a source of energy for doing good and helpful things that will outlive you. You are motivated by a driving force to produce transformational, lasting change.

STRATEGIC

The Strategic theme enables you to sort through the clutter and find the best route. It is not a skill that can be taught. It is a distinct way of thinking, a special perspective on the world at large. This perspective allows you to see patterns where others simply see complexity. Mindful of these patterns, you play out alternative scenarios, always asking, "What if this happened? Okay, well what if this happened?" This recurring question helps you see around the next corner. There you can evaluate accurately the potential obstacles. Guided by where you see each path leading, you start to make selections. You discard the paths that lead nowhere. You discard the paths that lead straight into resistance. You discard the paths that lead into a fog of confusion. You cull and make selections until you arrive at the chosen path — your strategy. Armed with your strategy, you strike forward. This is your Strategic theme at work: "What if?" Select. Strike.

Scriptures that relate to the Strategic theme:

So many gathered around that there was no longer room for them, not even in front of the door; and he was speaking the word to them. Then some people came, bringing to him a paralyzed man, carried by four of them. And when they could not bring him to Jesus because of the crowd, they removed the roof above him; and after having dug through it, they let down the mat on which the paralytic lay.
Mark 2:2-4

Make me to know your ways, O LORD;
teach me your paths.
Lead me in your truth, and teach me,
for you are the God of my salvation;
for you I wait all day long.

Psalms 25:4-5

It is not good to have zeal without knowledge, nor to be hasty and miss the way.

Proverbs 19:2 (NIV)

No testing has overtaken you that is not common to everyone. God is faithful, and he will not let you be tested beyond your strength, but with the testing he will also provide the way out so that you may be able to endure it.

1 Corinthians 10:13

For further understanding of your talents, examine these five insights and select those that describe you best.

☐ You create multiple ways to do things.

☐ You can quickly pick out the relevant issues and patterns when confronted by problems and complexities.

☐ You have a "What if this happens?" mentality toward work and life. This type of questioning helps you see, plan, and prepare for future situations.

☐ Some may criticize you for not moving on issues as quickly as they may like, but you know that there is great wisdom in reviewing all of the potential problems and searching for the alternative that will work best.

☐ Strategic talents are valuable because they enable you to quickly reach goals by seeing the pros and cons of various alternatives. You carefully consider the whole picture and then generate the most effective set of actions or routes to take.

WOO

Woo stands for winning others over. You enjoy the challenge of meeting new people and getting them to like you. Strangers are rarely intimidating to you. On the contrary, strangers can be energizing. You are drawn to them. You want to learn their names, ask them questions, and find some area of common interest so that you can strike up a conversation and build rapport. Some people shy away from starting up conversations because they worry about running out of things to say. You don't. Not only are you rarely at a loss for words, you actually enjoy initiating with strangers because you derive satisfaction from breaking the ice and making a connection. Once that connection is made, you are quite happy to wrap it up and move on. There are new people to meet, new rooms to work, new crowds to mingle in. In your world there are no strangers, only friends you haven't met yet — lots of them.

Scriptures that relate to the Woo theme:

Do not neglect to show hospitality to strangers, for by doing that some have entertained angels without knowing it.
Hebrews 13:2

When he saw the crowds, he had compassion for them, because they were harassed and helpless, like sheep without a shepherd. Then he said to his disciples, "The harvest is plentiful, but the laborers are few; therefore ask the Lord of the harvest to send out laborers into his harvest."
Matthew 9:36-38

Conduct yourselves wisely toward outsiders, making the most of the time.
Colossians 4:5

For further understanding of your talents, examine these five insights and select those that describe you best.

- ☐ You have the capacity to quickly connect with people and generate positive responses from them.
- ☐ You can enter a crowd of people and easily know what to do and what to say.
- ☐ You see no strangers, only friends you haven't met yet.
- ☐ Because you know so many people, some may believe that you form only shallow relationships. Others, however, will envy the way you make friends.
- ☐ Woo talents are valuable because people are influenced by your ability to draw them into a group or relationship.

CHAPTER 3

Using Your Talents for Growth and Service

You've learned about the talents associated with each of your five Signature Themes. Are you wondering how to apply these talents in your congregation and in your life? Actually, they already play a part in the choices you make every day. It just happens naturally.

Consider Bob, Kathy, Donna, and Ray, who are all going on a two-week trip to the Holy Land with a group from their church. Bob has Context as a Signature Theme, so it's not surprising that the first thing he does in preparation for the journey is study the history of the region. He wants to understand the roots of the current situation in Jerusalem.

One of Kathy's Signature Themes is Woo, so one of her goals for the trip is to befriend everyone else who is going. In her world there are no strangers, only new friends yet to be met. She expects to come home from this trip with 25 new pals.

Donna's Signature Themes include Discipline, so she wants a detailed itinerary. She must know what to pack and what to expect each day.

Ray, on the other hand, has Adaptability as one of his Signature Themes. He isn't at all bothered by the fact that the travel plans aren't going to be finalized until three days before they leave. He won't mind if the daily schedule gets changed (which it no doubt will). In fact, he looks forward the exciting changes that each new day will bring.

Your greatest talents don't come into play only during life's big events — you use them every day. Do you set out your clothes the night before, or do you decide what to wear just before you get dressed in the morning? Do you try something new on the menu when you go to a restaurant, or do you simply order the same thing most of the time? Do you make quick decisions about what movie to see or book to read, or do you ponder and weigh options first? Do you talk to the people in line with you at the grocery store, or do you flip through a magazine? Your talents filter the way you approach every single situation you encounter and every decision you make.

Your talents also influence how you grow spiritually and the ways you serve God and others through your church. If the new-member coordinator had taken the time to help Rick, the disgruntled greeter from Chapter 1, identify his talents and assume a role that built on those talents, Rick's church would have gained a more loyal, spiritually productive member.

Knowing your talents when you join a new church can help you avoid the pitfalls of serving in a role that doesn't quite fit. When you know your talents, you naturally try to find ways to live them out.

Phil understands this. When he was growing up, his family belonged to a very strict church. "You couldn't dance, you couldn't listen to rock and roll music, you couldn't go to the skating rink because they played rock and roll music, you couldn't go to the bowling alley because they drank there, you couldn't go shoot pool," he recalls. "There were so many things you couldn't do, and so I grew up left out of a lot of things. Kids would have parties, and of course I couldn't go."

Includer is Phil's top Signature Theme, so he reaches out to everyone — he doesn't want anyone to feel left out like he did growing up. Phil's personal mission is "to look for the wall-flowers, or the old people who are sitting by themselves, or the handicapped, or those who are not included — and include them."

Phil says he tries "to show love across the board to all people," and his upbringing had a big part in that. "But," he continues, "my desire to reach out to practically everyone is obviously a natural part of me. I just love people."

Your talents also influence the way you approach your growth and study. This is especially true in your study of the Scriptures. One of Sarah's Signature Themes is Individualization, and that influences how her faith has grown. "I think the way I studied the

Bible and learned from it was through its characters," she says. She appreciates the uniqueness of those characters and seeks inspiration from them. "I love the story of Esther; I love the story of Joseph; I love the story of Paul." But her favorite Bible character is Esther. "I love the whole story, how she was a nothing and became the queen. With great courage, this woman of nothingness went before the king to save her people, even though she didn't want to do it. But she did. She drew her belief from the bottom of her being, and with the support of others, through prayer and fasting, and asking God to make a way for her, she went. So when I am facing a difficult task, I think of Esther, and she becomes my courage."

FOCUS ON OUTCOMES

Phil and Sarah are effectively putting their talents to work in their spiritual lives. They know how to find fulfillment. You might be tempted to imitate them. But beware: One of the most common mistakes people make in their spiritual lives is to focus on the *steps to spiritual growth* rather than on the *outcomes of spiritual growth*. Often, people will look at the lives of spiritually mature individuals and try to replicate the steps these individuals took to achieve maturity in their own lives.

The mistake is assuming that if two people follow the same steps, pattern, or procedures, they will produce the same outcomes in their lives. This goes against everything that Gallup's talent research reveals. You may want to achieve the outcome of spiritual maturity, but the steps you take to successfully achieve that goal will depend greatly on your unique talents.

Let us illustrate. One of the goals for all the members of Brian's church is for their faith to be involved in every aspect of their lives. Intellection is one of Brian's Signature Themes, so he has to think about things — a lot. He needs to take time to ponder and ruminate on concepts, and not only that, he is constantly thinking about all manner of topics. "The best way for me to reach this goal," Brian says, "and I think it's an important goal for all Christians, is to start each day by reading the Bible and also some thought-provoking, challenging books about spiritual concepts. Then I can think about what I've read throughout the day, and I think to myself, 'How does what I studied this morning relate to what I'm doing right now?' This really helps me pay attention and think about my faith more deeply."

Shauna is a member of the same church, and she takes a different approach. "I found out that I have Activator as one of my Signature Themes, and that really explained a lot to me. I always found Bible studies where you just sit around and read the Bible and just talk about it really, really boring," she says.

Shauna used to feel guilty about this, until she learned that Activators can get bored easily. They have to *do* something for their faith to grow, not just *talk* about something. "So I got involved in delivering meals to the elderly and homebound, and because I'm actually doing something for someone and I can see the results, I've found that I'm really starting to grow in my faith. I just need to be involved in doing something meaningful, and I find that involvement spills out into every other area of my life." Now, instead of feeling guilty about her talents, she feels good about the way her talents help her make a difference in the lives of others.

Both Brian and Shauna are achieving their goal — making faith central to every aspect of their lives — but they are doing it in very different ways. The outcome is the same for both, but the steps they take to reach the outcome are different — because they have different talents.

USING TALENTS TO FORGIVE

Your talents determine how you approach problem solving in your spiritual life. Take the doctrine of forgiveness. How you forgive others depends a great deal on your talents. "I've always been the type of person who gets my feelings hurt easily," recalls Melissa. Because of that, she has always found it hard to forgive people who have hurt her deeply. "I used to feel like a failure as a Christian, because we're supposed to forgive, right? Because God forgave us in Jesus' death and resurrection, we're supposed to forgive others. When I found out that I had a lot of talent in

Empathy, it all made sense — I could so strongly feel others' emotions toward me in those hurtful situations, and because of my empathy, it was hard to let go of those feelings."

But then Melissa figured out a way to help her forgive and get past the hurt. "Usually, when people find out they've hurt me," she says, "they're sorry about it and feel pretty bad about it. So instead of focusing on my feelings about it, I focus on theirs. I imagine what they must feel like. I put myself in their shoes and know how bad I would feel if I hurt someone I cared about. Putting myself in their position and feeling their feelings helps me get past my own hurt and move on to forgiveness."

Craig, on the other hand, has always been quick to forgive others. His Harmony talents certainly are the key. "I just want people to get along," he says, "and I want to get along with everybody, too. But I'm not a doormat, either — I also have a lot of Command. I know that seems like a weird combination, but it's how I approach the world." When he feels wronged or hurt by someone, Craig can confront the situation or the person fairly quickly. Not one to hold a grudge, he can forgive quickly too. "I want to resolve the issue so that we can get the relationship back on track," he says. "Letting things fester only makes matters worse and makes it harder for people to get along with each other. Forgiveness helps restore the peace."

Forgiveness is a central doctrine and expectation of the Christian faith. But the way Christians forgive — the steps to the outcome — depends on their unique combination of talents. To grow spiritually and live the life God intends you to live, you need to focus on the outcomes you want to achieve and let your talents determine the best way to get there.

Your talents are a precious gift from God. They influence how you see, experience, and make your contribution to the world. The following pages list insights, thought-provoking questions, and action suggestions that can help you build on your talents to create and apply strengths — and to grow spiritually and serve God and others in the process. Choose those that you feel best match your talents and values, and put them to use as you develop your personal plan for growth and service.

ACHIEVER

If you are particularly talented in Achiever, you have a great deal of stamina and work hard. You take great satisfaction from being busy and productive.

☐ Participate in a "Year Through the Bible" program. You will feel great satisfaction and growth as you check off each day's reading and see what you have accomplished at the end of the year.

☐ Make a prayer list of people, events, and situations you are concerned about. Pray through this list at least once a day.

☐ Ask to serve in a leadership position in your church. Your drive to achieve will help the groups you lead accomplish a great deal.

☐ Volunteer to organize a mission project for your church — locally or internationally. Set goals for the mission team, and keep track of your accomplishments.

☐ Volunteer to be a resource for your church's annual planning retreat. You will be able to help break down abstract dreams into achievable goals with measurable milestones.

☐ What is your idea of spiritual maturity? What characteristics of spiritual maturity have you seen in others? Make a list of your goals for spiritual maturity, and keep track of your progress on achieving those goals.

☐ You like to work hard, and you appreciate the hard work of others. When getting involved in a church project, choose to work with other hard workers. As you and your team create common goals, you will feel great satisfaction in achieving those goals together — and create a common bond.

☐ Accept that you might be discontented even when you achieve. Because of who you are, this is God's way of nudging you forward. As you focus on your spiritual growth, your internal "need to achieve" will keep pushing you to grow.

☐ Because for you every day starts at zero, you need to remind yourself to celebrate what you have accomplished. Take a moment to appreciate your successes. You can look ahead tomorrow. Today, celebrate. Even God took time to stop and say, "It is good" multiple times when He created the universe.

☐ Be careful not to let your "list" take ultimate priority. Remember that your list is your means of achieving your goals — it is not the goal itself. Count personal achievements in your scoring "system." This will help you direct your Achiever talents toward your family, friends, and spiritual life in a positive way.

ACTIVATOR

If you are particularly talented in Activator, you can make things happen by turning thoughts into action. You are often impatient.

☐ Find a cause that really means something to you. If your church is already involved in supporting this ministry, get involved. If it is not, you are the perfect person to get it started.

☐ Keep a log of your accomplishments each day or week. As a particularly talented Activator, you know you will be judged not by what you say, not by what you think, but by what you make happen.

☐ Consider partnering with church friends who are exceptionally talented in Strategic, Analytical, or Futuristic. They will help you look around the corner and plan ahead.

☐ Try to work on only action-oriented teams. Typical church committees will bore you. Your sense of urgency can be a key factor in effecting change.

☐ Take responsibility for your intensity by always asking for action when you are part of a group. You have the talent to help a group work around obstacles.

☐ If you have exceptional Relator or Woo talents along with your Activator, you may be an excellent recruiter of new members or Sunday school teachers.

☐ Seek opportunities to make your own decisions and act on them. In particular, look for start-up situations, like beginning a new ministry, program, or class. You also can be helpful in reviving programs that have lost their spark but are still important to the mission of your church.

☐ Your spiritual growth will come more from doing than from discussing or thinking. Recognize that traditional Bible studies might bore you — and don't let others make you feel guilty about it. You will grow best from putting biblical principles into action, like volunteering your time to work in a homeless shelter, going on a short-term mission trip to build a school in Central America, or working in a free clinic.

☐ Others might dismiss you as impatient and label you a "ready, fire, aim" person. So was Peter — and Jesus chose him as a leader, saying, "You are Peter, and on this rock I will build my church" (Matthew 16:18a). Recognize, however, that you may make some mistakes along the way, and be prepared to apologize and fix them. Also consider partnering with people who are particularly talented in themes such as Strategic, Deliberative, or Responsibility. Their talents can help you prevent these mistakes.

☐ Recognize that your "pushiness" might sometimes intimidate others. You can soften this by remembering that it is through relationships that God works best: Don't let your desire for action ruin your relationships.

ADAPTABILITY

If you are particularly talented in Adaptability, you prefer to "go with the flow." You tend to be a "now" person who takes things as they come and discovers the future one day at a time.

☐ You like change. You might be at your best when you take on short-term, spur-of-the-moment roles in the church that need to be filled quickly. One week, you might give a regular Sunday school teacher a break by agreeing to substitute, and the next week might find you volunteering to serve refreshments following a funeral, or offering your basement floor to an out-of-state youth group that needs a place to sleep.

☐ Many people see last-minute requests as interruptions. Being the adaptable person that you are, you see them as beautifully disguised opportunities for service. Let people know that it is never too late to ask for your help.

☐ You live in the moment. Not yesterday, not tomorrow — *today*. You want to be fully immersed in the here and now. In order for you to grow, you need to focus on how your faith is lived in each moment. It is not reflections on the past or discussions about the future, but the experiences of the present that make your heart beat fast.

☐ Don't make commitments that are too far into the future. The further you are from the present, the less you are likely to be engaged. What occasionally looks like procrastination might actually be your high levels of Adaptability talent.

☐ Your best service will be in your church's most dynamic and changing environments. Depending on your other dominant areas of talent, it could be caring for toddlers in the nursery, directing traffic in the church parking lot, fielding calls on a 24-hour suicide hotline, or taking care of customers at your church's food pantry.

☐ While you don't necessarily have a strong preoccupation with or appreciation for tomorrow, your ability to fully experience the present may assist those who are planning and preparing for the future. Your keen awareness of the present situation can help clarify their plans for future improvement.

☐ Avoid roles in your congregation that demand structure and predictability. These roles will quickly frustrate you, make you feel inadequate, stifle your independence — and limit your opportunities to do what you do best.

☐ Cultivate your reputation as a calm and reassuring person when others become upset by daily events. Because change is your "friend," you can help others adapt to and live with the changes that are bound to come into their lives.

☐ Help those around you appreciate the moment. Help them treasure the present as a precious gift from God. God is not just God of the past and future, but also God of the present. Eternity begins now.

☐ In your Bible study, pay particular attention to the times when God surprises people. You will understand the wonder and joy such surprises can bring, and reading about the God of surprising change will deepen your faith and enhance your spiritual journey.

ANALYTICAL

If you are particularly talented in Analytical, you search for reasons and causes. You have the ability to think about all the factors that might affect a situation.

☐ Look for tangible evidence and data that validate your faith. Develop a logical explanation that can be shared with others who seek the truth.

☐ Develop your question-asking talents. Great questions could lead you to great personal and spiritual discoveries.

☐ Participate in a congregation that not only allows, but even encourages you to blend your faith and your intellect.

☐ You are more apt to act with commitment when you are convinced of something. Ask questions and do research that will help you to give a definitive *yes* or *no*.

☐ When a situation is charged with emotion, offer the logic of your cool head.

☐ Don't be afraid to express your skepticism. It will bring validity and reality to any discussion of what could be. Make sure your analysis is delivered in a positive and helpful manner.

☐ Intensely research a faith concept or topic that is personally relevant and that you are passionate about. By thoroughly analyzing the subject, your faith will grow stronger and deeper.

☐ You long to see improvement and growth in your congregation, but in your mind such progress will never be the result of jumping to conclusions or jumping on the bandwagon. You can help others take a more thoughtful, responsible, and organized approach to the future.

☐ Continue to use your Analytical talents to think about the important numbers in your congregation. What patterns or trends are obvious to you? When you are convinced of something, you tend to become a committed and articulate advocate.

☐ When serving in decision-making roles in your congregation, identify credible, reliable sources. You are at your best when you have well-researched sources of information and numbers to support your logic. For example, determine the most helpful books, Web sites, or publications that can serve as references.

ARRANGER

If you are particularly talented in Arranger, you can organize, but you also have a flexibility that complements this ability. You like to figure out how all of the pieces and resources can be arranged for maximum productivity.

☐ Think about all that God enables you to be a part of. Think about all that you accomplish in a day. Take the time to thank God for helping you do all that you do.

☐ How many different things do you like to have going on at one time? How much can you take on in the church and still be effective? You love to "juggle," but to ensure that you maintain quality, know the volume of projects or responsibilities you can handle and still maintain quality.

☐ Volunteer your multitasking abilities. Serve on church committees that take on large projects you can help manage. With your ability to see the most efficient way to complete projects, you may not be happy simply carrying out others' tasks. Join a steering committee or group that helps make decisions.

☐ How can you help someone who is overwhelmed by all of his or her tasks? Help bring calm to people or situations. Let them know how you envision things working out. You may see it more clearly than they are able to.

☐ Your talent with logistics could make you very helpful in running the operations for your church or organization. Seek roles in these areas.

☐ If you are talented in working with numbers, consider volunteering to work with the financial operations of your church. Your Arranger talents can help you find ways to make sure projects and programs can happen without financial obstacles.

☐ The fact that you are flexible doesn't mean that your priorities and values are constantly changing. When challenged, explain that your values and priorities remain the same, but that you are simply looking for better ways to implement them.

☐ Know and understand the mission, vision, and values of your congregation. With your talents, you can help your church's leaders find new and better ways to more effectively accomplish the mission.

☐ Your spiritual growth probably won't follow a set routine, even though you may make daily time for your growth. You will constantly try different methods, programs, and strategies, finding what works best for you at the moment. As your life circumstances change, however, so will your spiritual growth practices.

☐ In your Bible study, pay particular attention to stories of how God and others find a "better way." From Creation to

Covenant, from Cross to Resurrection, from the apostle Paul to a "new heaven and earth," the Bible is full of examples of finding better ways to reach individuals with God's life-changing love. Your strengths and your spiritual growth will be affirmed by these stories.

BELIEF

If you are particularly talented in Belief, you have certain core values that are unchanging. Out of these values emerges a defined purpose for your life.

☐ How much of your day, week, month, or year is spent on those things you value? Reflect on how your beliefs affect the way you prioritize your time.

☐ Your faith in the things you value and believe is reassuring to others who may have doubts or who are indecisive. Spend time sharing your views with others in a nonthreatening way.

☐ Do your values affect your job? Working for a religious organization that promotes and shares your beliefs would enable you to freely express and live your values. Avoid any occupation or company that is inconsistent with your values or would force you to compromise them.

☐ What principles and values has the Bible reinforced for you? Write down the five most important lessons you've learned from the stories of the Bible. Ask others close to you to write down their list and share your similarities and differences.

☐ Walk the talk. In the last 24 hours, how did you live out the purpose you were put on Earth for? In the next 24 hours, how will you live out the purpose God intended for you?

☐ Think about a particular spiritual speaker or sermon that helped solidify your beliefs. What did this experience teach you? How was the message delivered? Share that lesson and the message with someone who might be unclear in his or her faith.

☐ Think about a specific situation in which someone held a view different from your own. How did you respond? Are you inquisitive, accepting, judging, critical? How can you be firm in your own beliefs without putting down those of others?

☐ Who is a spiritual role model for you? What do you admire about this person? Think about how you can be a spiritual role model for others, and take steps to do exactly that.

☐ Clarify your values by thinking about one of your best days ever. How did your values play into the satisfaction that you received from your best day? How can you organize your life to repeat that day as often as possible?

☐ Discover the circumstances in which you feel most comfortable sharing your strongest beliefs. Would you be best able to share your core beliefs by being a church leader or Sunday school teacher or by participating in a short-term mission project? Are the ways you are serving your church consistent with your deepest beliefs about the most effective way to witness your faith?

COMMAND

If you are particularly talented in Command, you have presence. You can take control of a situation and make decisions.

☐ When the going gets tough, the tough get going. If a crisis or conflict emerges in your church, get involved. People will probably look to you in times like these, and tough times will often bring out the best in you.

☐ Look for opportunities to lead. You are likely to be most comfortable and effective in the driver's seat. Others will follow you because your emotional strength provides confidence and inspiration, and your decision-making capacity will often provide clarity and direction.

☐ You will often dare to say what others only have the courage to think. In your mind, things are easier to deal with when they are up front and out in the open, so you tell it like it is. Think about situations in which the truth must be told. You are probably one of the people best equipped to tell it.

☐ You have a natural emotional power that can be explosive, that is, the power to move undesirable obstacles and barriers out of the way. Explosions can be constructive or destructive. A constructive explosion moves things that are stuck or impeding progress. What obstacles and barriers are impeding the progress of a person's faith or of your church's ministry? Where could you detonate a strategically placed explosion?

☐ As someone who knows how to get tough, you might want to think about how you can occasionally add some tenderness to your toughness. Not every situation will be a crisis or a conflict that requires the explosiveness of your emotional power and intensity. Do you have other talents that will complement your courage with tenderness and keep your assertiveness from turning aggressive or offensive?

☐ Study some of the stories in the Bible that teach about courage and cowardice. They will help you understand the value of the gift you have and the responsibilities that come with it.

☐ Ask people for their opinions. Sometimes your candor will prove intimidating, causing others to tread very lightly for fear of your reaction. Watch for this. If necessary, explain that you are candid simply because it feels so uncomfortable to keep things bottled up, not because you want to frighten other people into silence.

☐ Take opportunities in your church to speak plainly and directly about sensitive subjects. Your unwillingness to hide from the truth can become a source of strength and constancy for others in your congregation. Strive to become known as a candid person.

☐ Find a cause you believe in and support it. You might discover yourself at your best when you are defending a cause in the face of resistance.

☐ With Command comes presence. You can make people believe they can do what others say is impossible. Your Command talents can be valuable assets in times when your church is called on to reach a lofty goal.

COMMUNICATION

If you are particularly talented in Communication, you generally find it easy to put thoughts into words. You are a good conversationalist and presenter.

☐ Volunteer to communicate the vision for the future to your congregation. Your ability to paint the future in a story will transcend the details that others dwell on and will inspire the audience to commitment and action.

☐ As part of your spiritual growth plan, keep a journal. Each day, record the way you saw God at work in your life. Your talents will enable you to give vivid details of God's activity in everyday events.

☐ Ask to be among those who read from Scripture during services. Using the same talent with which you make your everyday stories rich and colorful, bring life and excitement to the story or passage you are asked to recite.

☐ For you, the best way to share your faith with others is through stories — stories of how you have seen God work in your life and in others' lives. Share your beliefs through stories that could be told for generations to come.

☐ The Bible is full of colorful, dramatic stories. Read them, learn them, and claim them as gems for your treasure chest. Remember them, tell them, and muse upon them when your life takes on a similar hue. They will most certainly serve as a source of comfort, encouragement, and inspiration to you.

☐ If your Communication talents are expressed through writing, volunteer to write devotional pieces for your church during special times of the year. Your talents will help others deepen their faith and commitment.

☐ Practice your presentations. Your opportunities to speak about matters of faith are of utmost importance. Improvisation has a certain appeal, but in general, an audience will respond best to a presenter who knows where he or she is headed. Counterintuitively, the more prepared you are, the more natural your improvisations will appear.

☐ Volunteer to collect stories and illustrations for your pastor to use in sermons. Find out the sermon topics for the month, and find stories that relate to the central themes.

☐ Often, an idea or a plan is best understood through a story. You can be the one to break up the "logjams" in church meetings by telling a story that encapsulates the essential points of the plan and enables people to move forward.

☐ Start a collection of stories or phrases that resonate with you. For example, cut out magazine articles that move you, or write down powerful word combinations. Practice telling these stories or saying these words by yourself, out loud. Listen to yourself actually saying the words. Refine.

COMPETITION

If you are particularly talented in Competition, you measure your progress against the performance of others. You strive to win first place and revel in contests.

- ☐ Develop a method to measure, count, or rank your spiritual growth.
- ☐ Think of your spiritual life as a race. Where are you in the race? Who ahead of you would you like to catch? What will it take?
- ☐ Keep a journal to record your personal spiritual victories.
- ☐ Use your drive to win to secure an important victory over injustice or evil.
- ☐ Keep track of the spiritual victories in your congregation and make them public. In your world, there is no victory without celebration.
- ☐ You know that progress must be measured to be meaningful. That's why you may be a key contributor as your church determines its most important measures of effectiveness. After the benchmarks have been determined, you can help your church improve by measuring against those benchmarks.
- ☐ Resist the temptation to assess your value — and that of others — by comparing your talents with theirs. We are

each created in the image of God, and each person's talents are a valuable asset to your church, whether they are in setting and exceeding goals or in tuning into the feelings of someone who is hurting.

☐ Let people know that being competitive does not equate with putting other people down. Your competitiveness can raise everyone's level of performance, focusing them on doing something great for God.

☐ Help your congregation identify its true competition. Who or what are you fighting to defeat, and who or what are you striving to catch and emulate?

☐ Take a group from your congregation to a church in your area that is considered a leader in some aspect of the faith. Compare their situation to yours, and help your church develop ways to improve.

CONNECTEDNESS

If you are particularly talented in Connectedness, you have faith in the links between all things. You believe there are few coincidences and that almost every event has a reason.

☐ Serve as the interdenominational link between prayer groups in your community. In a spirit of ecumenism, exchange prayer requests. Enlist members of churches, synagogues, and mosques to pray for one another's needs, for understanding that goes beyond tolerance, and for peace in the world.

☐ Pray for peace, first in your own heart, then in the hearts of your brothers and sisters — especially those whose decisions dramatically influence the lives of others. Include leaders of nations, armies, and diplomatic corps.

☐ Join or start a prayer chain. Pray for those who request prayers for themselves, their family, their friends, and for the entire human family.

☐ Create a solitude experience. Spend one day, a weekend, a week, or more away from the distractions of daily life. During your time away, simply "be." Slow down. Look. Listen. Notice. Seek God in this sacred quiet space.

☐ Visit members of your congregation who cannot attend services. Reach out to the homebound, nursing home residents, the sick, the overwhelmed caregiver, the single parent, or the unemployed. Simply spend quality time with them. Listen attentively; be present.

☐ Explore leading a Bible study group. Your Connectedness talents might naturally equip you to see connections between the Biblical world and the modern world, and to readily perceive ancient lessons that are still applicable today.

☐ Pay attention to print and broadcast media for news about people around the world or in your community who are suffering, struggling, grieving, rescuing, or providing medical assistance and humanitarian aid. Remember these people in your daily prayers as you go about your studies, work, play, or relaxation.

☐ Communicate by telephone, e-mail, or mail with members of your church who are in the military, imprisoned, away at school, or for other reasons temporarily living far from their congregation. You can help them feel connected even when they are not physically present.

☐ Start or expand a recycling program or a soil or water conservation program in your congregation. This is a way for you to put your understanding of our connection to the environment into action.

☐ Organize or participate in a blood drive at your church. Giving blood is a relatively simple act with far-reaching consequences, saving lives of people you may never know.

CONSISTENCY

If you are particularly talented in Consistency, you are keenly aware of the need to treat people the same. You try to treat everyone in the world with consistency by setting up clear rules and adhering to them.

☐ Make a list of the rules of consistency by which you can live — your own set of "spiritual laws." These rules might be based on certain values that you have or on certain truths that you consider "non-negotiables" in your tradition. Counterintuitively, the clearer these rules, the more comfortable you will be with individuality within these boundaries.

☐ You will grow best in a faith environment where expectations are clearly defined and rules are equally enforced. How would you characterize your church with regard to expectations and rules?

☐ To you, rules are not heavy burdens, but helpful blessings. They keep you on the right track. What are the most critical rules that you follow to keep you on track spiritually?

☐ You are likely to have a higher standard than most with regard to keeping the rules. You may need to occasionally remind yourself that relationships are more important than rules and that rules are a means, not an end in themselves.

☐ You think people should be treated the same, and you are sensitive to inequality and injustice. Do you know someone in your community or congregation whose rights have been violated because of race, gender, age, socio-economic status, or education? How you could you be an advocate for this person or group?

☐ You probably will be more at home in situations and settings where concrete tasks are accomplished or policy decisions are being made instead of places where theoretical, abstract, or long-range discussions are taking place.

☐ You are better at thinking about the group than thinking about the individual. You see the forest better than you see the trees. Use your awareness of equality in the midst of diversity to help develop organizational policies and procedures that create a level playing field in your church.

☐ You think people should be treated the same. Could there be some exceptions to the rule? In what instances might individualization be more valuable than generalization? When might it be okay to say, "It depends"?

☐ Balanced and consistent, your even-keeled approach could have a calming and supportive effect on those who live chaotic lives. You might be a stable and solid pillar on whom others can lean.

☐ Cultivate a reputation in your congregation for pinpointing those who really deserve credit. Ensure that respect is always given to those who truly performed the work. You can become known as the conscience of your church.

CONTEXT

If you are particularly talented in Context, you enjoy thinking about the past. You understand the present by researching its history.

☐ Think back to what you were taught about God as a child. Ponder these questions: In what ways has your image of God remained basically the same? In what ways is it quite different?

☐ Study the history of your faith tradition, examining the lives of its key characters. How do their trials and tribulations, as well as their trust and faith in God, give you a model for how to live your life in the 21st century?

☐ Write your spiritual autobiography. Include photos of key events in your life. Create a timeline to illustrate turning points in your unique spiritual journey.

☐ Research the history of your church. Work alone or with others to write an account of your congregation. Interview the oldest members to capture their earliest memories of their place of worship. Collect photographs, newsletters, bulletins, architectural plans, member directories, and lists of pastors and other leaders. Consider publishing and selling this history as a fundraising project.

130

☐ Identify strained relationships or misunderstandings between individuals or groups within your church. As a first step toward reconciliation, identify and understand the events and factors that contributed to their "dis-ease" with each other. By truly listening and helping them understand how they arrived at their conflict, you can help individuals and groups resolve their differences.

☐ Serve on your congregation's anniversary celebration committee. Record living histories on audiotape, videotape, or DVD. Interview members of all ages as they prepare for, participate in, and remember the anniversary's events and their meanings.

☐ Teach or participate in a class that studies current events and relates those events to issues of faith. You will enjoy researching the history of the event to understand "how we got here," and sharing your knowledge with others will bring richness to the discussion.

☐ If you are teaching a class or leading a small group, build your lessons around case studies and stories from the Bible. You will enjoy the search for the appropriate case or Bible story, and those you teach will learn from these precedents. Use your understanding of the past to help others map the future.

☐ In your study of the Bible, be sure to read books about the history of the Bible — for example, the discovery of ancient texts, the ancient culture of the Middle East, how the Bible was authored, edited, and codified. Understanding the Bible's historical context will deepen your appreciation of the Bible's message for today.

☐ Be ready to accept change. Remember that God is not just the God of the past, but also of the present and the future. Context does not equate with "living in the past." Instead, you can actually become known as an active agent for positive change. Your Context talents should allow you to identify more clearly than most the aspects of the past that can be discarded and those that must be retained to build a sustainable future.

DELIBERATIVE

If you are particularly talented in Deliberative, you are best described by the serious care you take in making decisions or choices. You anticipate the obstacles.

☐ Identify the threats that could destroy your spiritual health or inhibit your growth. Take careful steps to come up with a plan that will protect you from those threats.

☐ Figure out how much time you need to make important personal decisions. Study one of your most successful decisions. What factors contributed to the success of that decision? Seek to replicate these factors in future decision making.

☐ Be a resource to groups that make important decisions. You can identify potential risks and pitfalls.

☐ Help others slow down long enough to consider all of the important details and factors that go into wise and responsible decision making.

☐ Intentionally play the role of "devil's advocate." Your questions will cause others to think and will ensure better decisions.

☐ Be intentional about getting to know those you live near or work closely with. Don't allow your cautious style to isolate you from relationships. This will take time for you, so make sure you allow for it.

☐ You believe that an ounce of prevention is worth a pound of cure. Consequently, you will usually be better at preventing than promoting. You are more apt to be guilty of sins of omission than sins of commission, so be careful not to let your cautious nature prevent you from taking action when you need to.

☐ Sometimes individuals and organizations lack restraint. That can be dangerous. You can be the brakes that slow down and prevent someone or something from a tragic crash.

☐ During times of change in your congregation, consider the advantages of being conservative when making decisions. Be ready to explain these advantages to others when asked.

☐ Whatever your role, take responsibility for helping others think through their decisions. Because you see details that others do not, you will soon be sought as a valuable sounding board.

DEVELOPER

If you are particularly talented in Developer, you recognize and cultivate the potential in others. You spot the signs of each small improvement and derive satisfaction from these improvements.

☐ You usually like it when others come to you for advice. Find positions in which you can be seen as a counselor to feed this internal need.

☐ Identify the people at church or in your spiritual groups whom you have helped. Tell them of the joy you received from helping them, and remind them that you are there for them in the future.

☐ Identify others who you believe are good "teachers." Ask them how they encourage others to grow and achieve. Try incorporating their methods into your own as you seek to build strengths as a developer.

☐ Think about the people in your church, Sunday school, or study groups whom you have seen succeed or achieve milestones. Recognize them for their accomplishments and help them think of new goals to strive for.

☐ How can you help your church, as a whole, develop? Ask your church leaders about their goals. Encourage and recognize them for leading the development of your church.

☐ If you like working with children, pick a Sunday school class to teach or assist. Would you enjoy being a youth group teacher or assistant? Think about how much joy you would receive seeing the spiritual development of your students.

☐ Ask you church leaders if there is a person in your church who could benefit from a spiritual mentor. Just having one-on-one time might be helpful to that person.

☐ List the last five people you have encouraged. Why did you encourage them? What motivated you? What methods of encouragement worked best? Learn from your successes.

☐ Find a way to mark progress in your spiritual growth. You will derive satisfaction as you see your progress because you know that even small steps in the right direction can yield big results over time.

☐ Because you are "wired" to notice progress in people, your pastor could benefit from your encouragement. Pastors sometimes feel that they see very little fruit of their efforts, and you have the talent to show your pastor how he or she is succeeding — even when success is not readily apparent.

DISCIPLINE

If you are particularly talented in Discipline, you enjoy routine and structure. Your world is best described by the order you create.

☐ Volunteer to be part of a cleaning day at your church. Help bring neatness and order to the area you are assigned.

☐ Volunteer to create a timeline, including celebrations of milestones for major projects in your church, such as a building fund campaign, Sunday school attendance recognition, or a "paintathon."

☐ Volunteer to keep the church calendar of events current and accurate.

☐ Make Bible reading and prayer part of your daily routine. You'll come to love the predictability, and you will grow spiritually as a result.

☐ In your Bible study, look for times when God brought order out of chaos. You'll see it in Genesis at the Creation, and you will see it all the way through to Revelation, when God returns to claim His own out of worldly chaos.

☐ Volunteer to help keep or organize your church's records. Your Discipline talents will make preparing the annual report much easier. In fact, you may enjoy preparing the report, gathering and organizing all the information so that it is a coherent whole.

☐ Recognize that mistakes might depress you. Precision is a core part of who you are; however, you must find ways to move through these moments of annoyance to prevent becoming discouraged.

☐ Recognize that others may not be as disciplined as you are. Sometimes, their processes will seem clumsy and disorganized to you. Try to look beyond the processes, and instead assess the results. Remember that even though God brought order out of chaos in Creation, the crowning achievement of Creation was fallible, unpredictable human beings.

☐ Learn the art of forgiveness, especially the art of forgiving yourself. Even though perfection is your goal, accept the fact that you and others will rarely reach perfection. Forgive and move on, celebrating the excellence achieved in spite of imperfection.

☐ Choose to serve on committees and join groups in the church that have structure and established routines. Groups and committees without well-defined processes and expectations will frustrate you.

EMPATHY

If you are particularly talented in Empathy, you can sense the feelings of other people by imagining yourself in others' lives or others' situations.

☐ Appreciate your gift for getting in touch with the thoughts and feelings of others. You can naturally build trust with others by telling them that you know how they are feeling.

☐ Spend time in silent prayer. It provides the potential for you to look within your soul and to experience your inner being. Simply observe your emotions and what goes on in your mind.

☐ Experiential worship will probably be most meaningful for you. For worship to move you, it must have an emotional connection. Look for this in your choice of congregations.

☐ Learn to recognize your own signs of being overly stressed, and know what to do about it. It is essential that you know when and how to make yourself a priority.

☐ Because you instinctively tune in to the feelings of others, you can assist those who have experiences of loss through death, divorce, or illness.

☐ Take the time to help, whether it's a stranger who needs directions, a child who needs extra attention learning how to read, or your aging neighbor who can't carry his groceries.

139

☐ Sponsor a child in a developing country. There are several organizations that coordinate such efforts. Ask your pastor for details.

☐ Know your limits. Don't push yourself beyond the healthy zone or the sanity zone. Keeping yourself in balance by knowing your limits is a big step toward keeping the world at large in balance.

☐ Jot down prayers and record insights from Bible readings. You may find that as you write, you hear God speaking in ways you had not heard before.

☐ Sometimes it is important to be silent. You have the talent to let other people understand that you know how they are feeling without talking. Over time, refine your nonverbal communication skills.

FOCUS

If you are particularly talented in Focus, you can take a direction, follow through, and make the corrections necessary to stay on track. You prioritize, then act.

☐ Start every day by giving thanks for all the people whose lives you will touch and whose lives will touch yours — from up-close or from a distance.

☐ Express gratitude for one, two, or three things that positively affected you during the day. Even on the worst of days, ask God to help you know when He was present in your life that day. This will help you refocus on the positive aspects of your life, aspects that in the long run will make you more effective.

☐ Participate in a "Year Through the Bible" program. You will feel great satisfaction and growth as you follow through on your commitment and see what you have accomplished at the end of the year.

☐ Volunteer to serve on committees or task forces that are charged with accomplishing a vast, complex goal. Your Focus talents will help others see the pertinent issues and keep the team on track.

☐ What are your goals for spiritual growth in the coming week, month, or year? Are the things you are doing and the way you are living helping you accomplish your goals? Your ability to prioritize will help you see the steps you need to take to reach your goal — eliminating the "excess baggage" along the way.

☐ Volunteer to serve on your church's outreach team. You will be able to help define goals for growth and set the priorities that will help the team reach those goals.

☐ Make a habit of praying at the same time each day. Whether it is five minutes or 50 minutes, set aside this time for yourself and God. Let prayer take a form that fits your style. Be open to changing how you use this time if you need variety. The key is to make a habit of fitting God into your day, whether it is in your quiet place at home, riding your bike, commuting to work, washing the dishes, or drinking a cup of coffee.

☐ Your greatest worth as a member of one of your church's teams or committees might be to help others set goals. At the end of each meeting, take responsibility for summarizing what was decided, for defining when these decisions will be acted on, and for setting a date when the group will reconvene.

☐ Take the time to write down your goals for spiritual growth, and refer to them often. You will feel more in control of your life this way. When you set your goals, discipline yourself to attach timelines and measurements. These will provide regular proof that you are indeed making progress.

☐ Identify your role models and "heroes of the faith." Write down in detail why you want to focus your life on similar kinds of actions, attitudes, and faithfulness.

FUTURISTIC

If you are particularly talented in Futuristic, you are inspired by the future and what could be. You inspire others with your visions of the future.

☐ Start or join a regular discussion of the future of your church. Ask others who are especially talented in Futuristic to join you. Meet once a month just to talk about the possibilities of your church's future. Be sure to include some people with strong Activator, Achiever, or Focus themes so that your shared vision can become a reality.

☐ Study the Bible, paying attention to God's promises related to the future — for your future, for future generations, for the future of the Church.

☐ Volunteer to talk about what you see as the future of your church. Your vision of the possibilities ahead will inspire others.

☐ Offer to help those who are experiencing difficult times. You can help them see a future of possibilities instead of the overwhelming present.

☐ When your congregation undertakes an ambitious project (like a building program) or is going through a major change (like a new senior pastor), you can set people's minds at ease by painting a vivid, hopeful picture of the future as a result of the project or change.

☐ Your vision of the future motivates you to work toward creating it, but remember that the future ultimately belongs to God. The disciples most certainly did not envision being called by Jesus, but God had other plans — and the disciples were open to the possibilities. Be proactive as you travel the road to your future, but be prepared for surprises God may present along the way — and be open to changing your plans.

☐ When you have an opportunity to describe your church's future in an article or a presentation, use as much detail as possible. Not everyone can intuitively see the future as clearly as you can.

☐ Don't get so wrapped up in thinking about and living in the promise of the future that you fail to appreciate the wonder of today. God is the God of all time and wants you to celebrate the present as well as plan for the future.

☐ When meetings get bogged down in "we've never done it that way before" talk, your vision of future possibilities can be a source of motivation for the group. The more vividly and hopefully you describe the future, the better people are able to move out of the past.

☐ Keep pictures, books, notes, or other reminders of what you are working toward where you will see them frequently. This will help you focus your talents and more effectively achieve your goals.

HARMONY

If you are particularly talented in Harmony, you look for consensus. You don't enjoy conflict; rather, you seek areas of agreement.

☐ You may experience spiritual satisfaction and growth by being involved in hands-on, practical projects in your congregation.

☐ While some people are energized by conflict and confrontation, such discord will cause you discomfort. You will flourish more with teachers and mentors who have a considerate and cooperative approach to learning than with those who tend to stir up controversy and rely on debate.

☐ You have a knack for smoothing out the bumps and creating more harmonious environments. How do you do this now? How could you do it better?

☐ Remember that harmony, not uniformity, is your goal. You instinctively understand that harmony cannot occur if everyone is "singing the same note." Help the people in the "choir" hear and appreciate the different parts that people "sing."

☐ You can see the common ground that links conflicted people. Be a key person in helping others understand what they already agree on. You will be more likely than others to notice commonalities.

145

☐ You are likely to be most open to growth when your life is balanced. Strive for internal harmony that exists between the competing demands and roles of your life.

☐ When you disagree with someone, you might find it difficult to express your thoughts and feelings. When is it most difficult for you to "speak the truth in love?" When is the truth more important than peace?

☐ You are sensitive to conflict. Who are the conflicted people around you? What are the conflicted areas in your congregation? Who might this information be important to?

☐ Don't let people in your church waste time and energy debating at the expense of important practical matters that must be taken care of. Your Harmony talents can help others focus on the truly important things about which they agree.

☐ Use your Harmony talents to build a network of people with differing perspectives that you can rely on when you need expertise. Your openness to these differing perspectives will help you learn.

IDEATION

If you are particularly talented in Ideation, you are fascinated by ideas. You are able to find connections between seemingly disparate phenomena.

☐ Write your own prayers to mark your joys and sorrows as well as your successes and failures. Jot down the date. Collect your favorite personal prayers and put them into a book.

☐ Spend time "musing" on spiritual things each day. This thinking time is very valuable to your growth, as your creative mind will find new ways to connect God to everyday living.

☐ Offer to teach a class that explores different religious traditions. Your Ideation talents will enable you to explain the complexities of these traditions clearly, and they will also help you see the connections between them.

☐ You will be a valuable member of any group, committee, or team that is charged with finding new ways to do things — from worship design, to community outreach, to redefining the congregation's organizational structure, to creating a new approach to teaching Sunday school. Your ability to help others see things from a different angle will help create new possibilities.

☐ In your study of the Bible, look for stories of innovation — the new "big ideas" that God introduced at different times in history. Seek to understand why the Christian movement was such a radical departure from the traditions of the time — and find an opportunity to share these insights with others.

☐ Whenever there is a disagreement or "logjam" in your congregation, you can help get things unstuck by looking at the situation from a different perspective, finding alternate solutions, and sharing what you see with those in leadership.

☐ Volunteer to help create meaningful services and liturgies for special celebrations and days of worship in your church. Weave a tapestry of music, readings, symbols, and quiet reflection time as well as prayers of praise, thanksgiving, and petition.

☐ Establish a practice of frequently journaling with God. Make this experience sacred by having a special journal and pen used only for this time with God. Dialogue with God — openly and honestly, trusting what flows from your pen onto the pages of your journal. Every couple of months, flip through your journal and read various entries. Look for recurring patterns, problems solved, and what created peace within you.

☐ Seek brainstorming sessions. There are bound to be teams in your church that are charged with creating new ways or improving existing ways of doing things — Sunday school curriculum design teams, building maintenance committees, strategic planning teams, outreach and mission teams, to name a few. With your abundance of ideas, you will make these sessions more exciting and more productive.

☐ You can become bored quickly, so make small changes in your spiritual life and your involvement in church activities and service opportunities. Experiment — try different ways of praying, attend a worship service that is a different style than the one you typically attend, get involved in a ministry that you've never done before. All of these will help keep you stimulated.

INCLUDER

If you are particularly talented in Includer, you are accepting of others. You show awareness of those who feel left out, and you make an effort to include them.

☐ For you, the Church is never an exclusive club for the chosen few. It is always an inclusive community where everyone is welcome. You might consider using your Includer talents to actively contact and welcome those outside your church and invite them to visit.

☐ When an outsider does come to your church, consider using your Includer talents to introduce this new person to some of the existing members of your congregation. You instinctively know that nothing makes an outsider feel more at home than knowing someone's name and having someone know his.

☐ As an Includer, you know that the best way to become a part of something is to get involved in it. You may play a key role in helping new people in your church move from spectators to participants, from consumers to contributors. You might be the perfect person to be involved in a newcomers' class designed to help individuals find their place.

☐ Your Includer talents may have more of a global, rather than local, flavor. You know that "God so loved the world" and that Jesus said, "Go into all the world." You have sensitivity toward those who may be left out. You might play a key role in encouraging diversity in the church by becoming a member of your church's mission team. Skin color, language, gender, age, or race should never keep people outside and apart from God.

☐ You probably have an instinctive awareness of exclusion. You know what it feels like to be left out. This awareness and understanding could be valuable to those who seek to create a more open and welcoming environment in their church, their class, or their small group. Maybe you could teach a class on the subject or let others know of your willingness to consult individually.

☐ Volunteer to assist with the implementation of a congregational survey. As an Includer, you want every voice to be heard, and a survey is a great way to make that happen.

☐ Whenever you go to a church event or meeting, consider yourself to be the designated greeter. Make it a point to talk to a new person before you talk to a friend or an acquaintance. This will probably come easily for you, and it will pull newcomers in.

☐ You naturally look for the best in people. Help your friends and fellow church members see what you see: that we are all created in the image of God and that God loves and values everyone.

151

☐ You might be a great advocate for global missions because you can see and explain what we all have in common. You can help others understand that to respect the differences among us (our diversity), you must begin by appreciating what we all share (our similarity).

☐ In your study of the Bible, pay particular attention to the stories and instances in which God and others welcome strangers and are advocates of the poor and oppressed. These passages will resonate with you, and your spiritual growth will be enriched by the God who is the friend of the poor and who welcomes the stranger.

INDIVIDUALIZATION

If you are particularly talented in Individualization, you are intrigued with the unique qualities of each person. You have a gift for figuring out how people who are different can work together productively.

☐ Establish a study group composed of people who possess different perspectives and different beliefs. The differences will fascinate you, and you will enjoy expanding your own viewpoints.

☐ Become a mentor to new church members. You have a knack for spotting what each new member enjoys, desires, and needs, and you can help each of them follow their own paths.

☐ Offer to be a task force leader. It is easy for you to figure out the right roles for each person based on individual talents and strengths.

☐ Become an expert in describing your own talents and strengths. What is the best way to grow in your faith? How do you learn best? Recognizing your own individuality will help you recognize others' uniqueness.

☐ Read the biographies of great spiritual leaders — or of ordinary people who have triumphed over impossible odds. You will be able to see how their unique talents made them successful.

☐ Offer to teach a class on the "great characters of the Bible." Your Individualization talents will make these characters come alive for your class.

☐ Your ability to see people one by one is a talent. Seek out opportunities to serve and lead in your church in which your Individualization talents can be appreciated and used. You might excel at counseling, supervising, teaching, writing human interest articles for your church newsletter, or serving on the nominating committee.

☐ Be ready to help others understand that true diversity can be found in the subtle differences between individuals, regardless of race, sex, or nationality. Because you know that human beings are "fearfully and wonderfully made" (Psalm 139:14), you can help people see the unique beauty in others.

☐ You may need to explain that it is appropriate, just, and effective to treat each person differently. Those with less Individualization talent might not see the differences among individuals and might insist that individualization is unequal and therefore unfair.

☐ Help your friends in your congregation become aware of each other's unique talents and needs. Soon people will ask you to help them understand another person's actions and attitudes.

INPUT

If you are particularly talented in Input, you have a craving to know more. You may very well like to collect and archive all kinds of information.

☐ Consider taking a trip to the Middle East or the Mediterranean. Your faith is likely to come alive as you actually see and experience the places in biblical history.

☐ Your natural inquisitiveness can help you be an outstanding researcher. Make yourself available to do research for those who need to speak or teach on topics about which they know little. Your resourcefulness will be valuable and helpful to such people as you provide them with interesting facts and relevant stories.

☐ You may already have a library of Christian books and resources that have enriched your own spiritual life. Consider developing a system that will enable you to share them with others.

☐ If your church has a library, you might enjoy volunteering there. If it doesn't, you might be a key person in getting one started.

☐ Your capacity for collecting and gathering might make you a natural contributor to your church's newsletter or Web site. You could help inform others about what is going on both inside and outside your congregation.

☐ In order to grow, you need to know. You need to know all about the faith tradition you are a part of. Reading about the particulars of your tradition, interviewing long-time members of your church, understanding all the factors that contributed to the watershed moments of Christianity — these will deepen your faith and enrich your spiritual life.

☐ Accept that you will never feel that you know enough — but don't let that paralyze you into inaction. Know how to determine when you know enough to act. Partnering with someone particularly talented in Activator or Achiever will help you accomplish great things for God.

☐ You will collect things that others will eventually need — from books to ideas to church information. Be ready to share.

☐ Identify situations in which you can share the information you have collected with other people. You could lead a small group or teach a class in your church. If you are not the leader, you could serve as a resource to enhance the topic or lesson with the knowledge you have gathered.

☐ In your Bible studies, compare various translations, learning about the translation process of each edition. The variances in meaning and differences in interpretation may fascinate you and deepen your appreciation of the Bible.

INTELLECTION

If you are particularly talented in Intellection, you are characterized by your intellectual activity. You are introspective, and you appreciate intellectual discussions.

- ☐ Schedule regular time for reflection, introspection, or meditation. This will be a fruitful time for you.
- ☐ Keep a list of the most important issues you are thinking about and/or the books you are reading.
- ☐ Record your thoughts on important concepts or issues, or communicate them to others, either verbally or in writing. This organization will lead to greater clarification of your thoughts and will prepare them for further development.
- ☐ Raise the deep and philosophical questions that others may not be aware of.
- ☐ Volunteer to review and recommend articles and books that are important for members of your congregation to read.
- ☐ Find partners who can help you turn your thoughts and ideas into practical and concrete action. Consider those who are especially talented in themes such as Activator, Strategic, and Achiever.
- ☐ Offer your thinking to primary teachers in your congregation. You will help them anticipate questions and achieve greater depth in their teaching.

☐ Take a yearly retreat for an extended period of solitude. You will return energized and ready to put your thoughts into action.

☐ Record your thoughts. It will help you clarify them, and it will prompt further thinking.

☐ Use your intellect to do an in-depth study of a critical issue or problem faced by your congregation.

LEARNER

If you are particularly talented in Learner, you have a great desire to learn, and you want to continuously improve. In particular, the process of learning, rather than the outcome, excites you.

☐ Participate in a Sunday school or Bible study class. Become an expert in your own religious beliefs and knowledgeable in the history and belief of other religions.

☐ Feed your constant need to learn through a Bible lesson for each day of the year.

☐ Share your knowledge in group seminars and workshops for your church or study groups.

☐ Start a book club with a religious premise. Center your group on educational and informative books about faith and spirituality. If Context is also one of your dominant areas of talent, you might also like books with a historical perspective.

☐ Keep track of what you have learned. Create a spiritual résumé of all you have learned and done. Share it with others so they may call on you as a resource.

☐ Ask what conferences or workshops are available for you to attend. Let others know you are willing to represent your church at these programs.

159

☐ You can be a catalyst for change in your church. Others might be intimidated by new ideas, new routines, or new circumstances, but your willingness to soak up this "newness" can calm their fears and spur them to participate. Take this responsibility seriously.

☐ Refine how you learn. For example, you might learn best by teaching. If so, seek opportunities in your congregation to teach a class or lead a small group. You might learn best through quiet reflection; if so, carve out this quiet time and "soak up" as much as you can about God.

☐ Find ways to mark the progress of your learning. If there are distinct levels or stages of learning within your spiritual growth program or the class you are taking, celebrate your progression from one level to the next. If no such levels exist, create them for yourself (for example, read five books on the apostle Paul, or make three presentations on new trends in Christian theology).

☐ Ask your pastor what theological or church management books he or she is reading, and read them as well. In doing so, you can fulfill your need to learn and also share what you've learned with your pastor, providing him or her with valuable feedback.

MAXIMIZER

If you are particularly talented in Maximizer, you focus on strengths as a way to stimulate personal and group excellence. You seek to transform something good into something superb.

☐ Consider how your talents and strengths relate to the mission in your life and how you can combine them to benefit your family, your church, or your community.

☐ Avoid serving on church committees that require continual problem solving — this will only frustrate you. You thrive not on fixing what's broken, but instead on taking what is working well and making it even better.

☐ Study success. Find out what has made the most successful churches, spiritual leaders, and ordinary people succeed.

☐ When you pray, thank God for the gifts you have, and ask for insights into ways that you can best use those gifts. How can God help you reach excellence? Creating excellence in your life, in the lives of others, and in your church is your gift to God.

☐ Offer to design a program for celebrating the successes of your congregation.

☐ Focus on your gifts. Are you musical? Are you a good speaker? Are you artistic? Do you love teaching others?

These are your best opportunities for mastery. Consider how your gifts and talents might best benefit your congregation.

☐ In group settings — committees, work teams, classes — help people recognize their own talents and strengths and those of others.

☐ Once you have identified your own talents and strengths, stay focused on them. Refine your skills, and add new ones. Acquire more knowledge. Practice. Keep working toward mastery — strength — in a few areas. Remember that God created the one and only you.

☐ Seek roles in your church in which you are helping other people succeed. In coaching, mentoring, or teaching roles, your focus on strengths will prove particularly beneficial to others. For example, because most people find it difficult to describe what they do best, start by arming them with vivid descriptions. Help them see how God uniquely created them.

☐ Spend time with people who have discovered their talents. The more you understand how marshaling talents leads to strengths and success, the more likely you will be to create strengths and success in your own life.

POSITIVITY

If you are particularly talented in Positivity, you have an enthusiasm that is contagious. You are upbeat and can get others excited about what they are going to do.

☐ Seek friends who love life as much as you do. They will uplift and support you.

☐ People who have negative or defeating attitudes and practices can drain you, but don't avoid them or withhold your Positivity from them. They need the lift you naturally provide!

☐ Start a collection of stories, positive sayings, and favorite Scriptures that will keep you focused on the positive when you are facing adversity. These positive examples can also help shift the tone when church meetings become gripe sessions.

☐ When others become discouraged or are reluctant to take risks, engage them in possibility thinking. Your attitude will provide the motivation to keep them moving.

☐ Help plan celebrations for your congregation. Your Positivity talents will help the planning team focus on fun.

☐ Choose opportunities for service in which you can encourage others, like Sunday school teaching, sponsoring new members, or prison ministry.

☐ When choosing Bible study groups or classes to join, select those in which the leader has a positive attitude, and in which fun is integrated with the learning. Too much seriousness brings you down and inhibits your growth. "The joy of the LORD is your strength." (Nehemiah 8:10)

☐ You tend to be more enthusiastic and energetic than most people. This is a very valuable talent you can bring to the life of your church. When others become discouraged or are reluctant to take risks, your attitude will provide the impetus to keep them moving. Over time, others will start to look to you for this "lift."

☐ Deliberately help others see God's blessings in their lives and the things that are going well for them. You can keep their eyes on the positive. Remember Paul's partner, Barnabas, whose name meant "son of encouragement" (Acts 4:36). Never underestimate the effect you can have on people.

☐ Be ready to explain that your enthusiasm is not simple naïveté. You know that bad things can happen — that there is suffering and tragedy in the world; you simply prefer to focus on the good things and on the positive ways God is working in the world. Pessimists might sometimes be right — but they are rarely the people through whom God accomplishes great things.

RELATOR

If you are particularly talented in Relator, you enjoy close relationships with others. You find deep satisfaction in working hard with friends to achieve a goal.

- ☐ How do you stay connected with people you have met — one on one or in groups? Be intentional about getting together or communicating with people from your church.

- ☐ When you are working with others, make time to get to know them personally. Set time aside after church to talk with fellow parishioners. You may not be comfortable initiating conversation, so be prepared with questions to ask.

- ☐ Who is the friend you've known the longest? Share and discuss your feelings and beliefs about spirituality with this person.

- ☐ Large study or worship groups may not feel comfortable to you. Arrange for smaller, more intimate classes in which your Relator talents will flourish.

- ☐ Volunteer to coordinate smaller social functions for people in your church.

- ☐ Remember to thank God and pray for your friends.

- ☐ Look for people with exceptional Woo talents in your surroundings. If you are hesitant to initiate relationships with others in your congregation, they can make initial connections that you can then take deeper. Call on their talents to help you when you are in a situation with stran-gers or people you don't know very well.

☐ Deliberately learn as much as you can about the people that you meet in your congregation. You like knowing about people, and other people like being known. You will be a catalyst for trusting relationships.

☐ Let your caring show. For example, help the members of a Sunday school class get to know each other better, or extend your relationships beyond church services.

☐ Remember that most life changes happen in relationships, and that one of the cornerstones of the Christian faith is God's desire for a relationship with each and every human being. Biblical stories of deep relationships, such as that between David and Jonathan, or between Jesus and his disciples, will be particularly meaningful to you.

RESPONSIBILITY

If you are particularly talented in Responsibility, you take psychological ownership of what you say you will do. You are committed to stable values such as honesty and loyalty.

☐ You need to "live" your faith to grow spiritually. Make a commitment to perform acts of neighborly love: delivering and serving meals at a homeless shelter, volunteering at a hospital, or relieving the caregiver of a hospice patient. Choose the commitments that are most meaningful to you.

☐ Join or start an accountability group made up of individuals who commit to holding each other accountable in their walk with God. Being held accountable by others and yourself is not something you dread, but rather is something you enjoy. You will grow through your accountability.

☐ Take personal responsibility for setting aside quality time to develop your relationship with God. Find the environment and the method that resonate with you most clearly, and set aside time for them each day. You will derive much satisfaction from following through on this commitment.

☐ For you, making a financial pledge to your congregation will be a powerful means of spiritual growth. Making a commitment and following through on it every week, knowing that you are funding the ministry of your church, will be a source of satisfaction and growth for you. If you are not doing so already, consider tithing — giving 10% of your income to your church.

☐ Be careful not to take on too much. You need to be able to follow through on each and every one of your commitments; otherwise, you will feel as if you have failed. Choose those areas of service in which you are talented and passionate.

☐ If you are also particularly talented in Woo or Activator, consider being a recruiter for various roles in your congregation. Your Responsibility talents will not let you rest until each role is filled with the right person.

☐ Take time to enjoy the completion of your commitments. Responsibility is a source of motivation for you, so it is important to appreciate the successes for which you are responsible.

☐ Consider fasting as a spiritual discipline. Identify opportunities in which fasting can unite you with the world's suffering people. Besides fasting from food, consider consciously abstaining from television, shopping, or other activities you enjoy to focus your attention on "the things of God."

☐ Figure out what pulls you away from God. When you have all the best intentions to make time for daily prayer,

Scripture reading, or meditation, what gets your attention instead? Work? Sleep? Television? Exercise? Shopping? Family? Friends? Household chores? Take personal responsibility for "clearing the clutter" and spending quality time with God.

☐ Start or join wellness activities in your church. Look to Scripture for connections between taking care of your body and taking care of your spirit. Taking responsibility for your physical health is a spiritual discipline, and when you feel better, you are happier.

RESTORATIVE

If you are particularly talented in Restorative, you are adept at dealing with problems. You are good at figuring out what is wrong and resolving it.

☐ Consider being a part of the lay-counseling ministry in your church. Tell people you are interested in their well-being and are eager to help them find solutions to their problems.

☐ Consider being a part of the lay-maintenance ministry in your church. Use your fix-it talents in the areas of greatest expertise for you, for example, structure, plumbing, heating/cooling, or lighting.

☐ Become an advocate for the disadvantaged in your congregation. Help make their needs known, and create opportunities for other members of your congregation to give of their time, talent, or other resources to help these individuals.

☐ As you study the Bible, pay particular attention to how men and women of faith dealt with their problems. The solutions that they discovered and implemented will be inspiring to you and a resource in your restorative efforts.

☐ Help start a food bank in your church, or arrange for contributions to your denomination's food bank.

☐ Your prayers will often focus on asking for guidance in solving problems — your own, those of others, and those of your community and world. As you open yourself up to God, you will find the solutions becoming clearer.

☐ Adopt a family in need for a period of time. Volunteer to help them get back on their feet.

☐ Your Restorative nature might lead you to be critical of your own talents. Give yourself a break, and recognize that your talents — your lesser talents as well as your greatest talents — are natural parts of you and cannot change. Try to redirect your Restorative attention toward "fixing" your areas of lesser skill and knowledge, which you *can* acquire. Accept the talents God has given you, and make the most of them.

☐ Sometimes the problems of the world's people might overwhelm you; if only you could "fix it all"! In those times, remember that the brokenness of the world cannot ultimately be fixed by you alone, but can be healed only by God.

☐ Sometimes the best way you can "fix it" is to allow other people to solve their own problems. You might want to rush in and solve things for them, but in so doing, you might hinder their learning. Often, the most important lessons we learn from God are those in which we find our own solutions.

SELF-ASSURANCE

If you are particularly talented in Self-Assurance, you feel confident in your ability to manage your own life. You possess an inner compass that gives you confidence that your decisions are right.

☐ When your internal voice speaks to you, listen. Reflect on where that instinct comes from. How does God speak to you through your own voice?

☐ Your confidence can be a source of inspiration for others. When others doubt their faith or direction, share how you came to your own decisions and beliefs.

☐ When volunteering for committees or projects, be careful of people or organizations that impose structure or direction on you. You usually don't appreciate others telling you what or how to do things.

☐ If you are also particularly talented in themes such as Communication or Belief, you may have the ability to be a powerful speaker. Discuss a passage or story from the Bible that is meaningful to you, and "persuade" others with your confidence about the lesson it teaches.

☐ Identify a person from whom you can seek spiritual advice when facing tough decisions. Because your exceptional Self-Assurance may lead you to rarely seek and always question advice, be sure this is someone who won't be offended if you don't accept his or her point of view. Honor this person by letting him or her know that you are usually very selective and rarely ask others for opinions.

☐ Do you know when to "go with God" and when to take control over those things within your power? Think about those things over which you have control and list them. Then think about those things that God has authority over. How do you let God work in your life?

☐ Think about when your intuition has been right and when it has been wrong. What was the difference? Was the "feeling" different? How can you hone your intuition?

☐ Share your Self-Assurance talents. Consider teaming with people who are especially talented in themes such as Developer, Strategic, or Futuristic, but who may not possess your high level of Self-Assurance. Your confidence can be the driving force that puts their development ideas for the church into motion.

☐ Realize that sometimes you will find it hard to put your certainty or intuition into words, possibly leading others to see you as self-righteous. Explain that your certainty does not mean that they should withhold their opinions. It might not seem like it to them, but you do want to hear their views. Your certainty at the moment doesn't mean that you are unwilling to accommodate their views.

☐ Help others find the positives in your certainty. Your Self-Assurance talents can give them confidence in God's care and providence during times of change, uncertainty, or trial.

SIGNIFICANCE

If you are particularly talented in Significance, you want to be very important in the eyes of others. You are independent and want to be recognized.

☐ Ask to help lead something big — very big — happening in your church. You'll enjoy the opportunity to be a part of something so significant.

☐ Use your expertise to help with a special project at your church. If you're a lawyer, be available to consult about legal advice. If you're a teacher, be available to facilitate a Sunday school teachers' in-service. If you're a human resources director, volunteer to chair the hiring committee.

☐ If your congregation has members share their faith journeys in worship services, volunteer to share yours. Your story can inspire others.

☐ Commit to giving a tithe (10% of your income) to your church. With a very small percentage of church members doing this, it sets you apart and honors God.

☐ As you study the Bible, pay close attention to the stories of the "heroes of the faith." How did they use their extraordinary talents and gifts for the benefit of their faith communities and the world? Their stories will inspire you to greatness.

☐ Don't be afraid to dream big dreams. Ask, "If time and money were no object, what great thing would I do for God?" Then set out to accomplish it, marking your milestones along the way.

☐ Write down your Signature Themes and refer to them frequently — they are gifts from God. Heightened awareness of your talents will give you the confidence you need to rebound, when, for whatever reason, your "audiences" are not giving you the feedback you need.

☐ Remember that in the ultimate scheme of things, it is God's "applause" and not the applause of others that truly counts. Sometimes, the things that you do to further your church's mission may go unnoticed by others — but God notices, and says, "Well done, good and faithful servant." And that is all that matters.

☐ Make a list of the spiritual goals you want to achieve, and post them where you will see them every day. Use this list to inspire yourself.

☐ Accept that, unless you possess exceptional Self-Assurance talents, you might fear failure. Don't let the fear of failure cause you not to act on God's behalf. Instead, use your fear as an opportunity to fully trust in God to achieve great things through you.

STRATEGIC

If you are particularly talented in Strategic, you create alternative ways to proceed. Faced with any given scenario, you can quickly spot the relevant patterns and issues.

☐ Look for opportunities to "step into" and "out of" committees and task forces that have their goals defined but need help identifying the steps for reaching the goals.

☐ Study the Bible for insight into how men and women of faith responded to life's challenges. Then, when you are faced with similar situations, you will have additional choices from which to sort and choose. Then you can move ahead.

☐ There are many options available for enhancing your spiritual growth — from books, to devotionals, to Bible-reading schedules, to "10 Easy Steps to _____." With all these options in mind, find what works best for you. Follow your intuition, and don't be afraid to change your strategy as new ideas come to your attention.

☐ You may be a good counselor for those facing difficult decisions. You can help them weigh their options and choose the best route.

☐ Volunteer to serve on your congregation's strategic planning team. Your natural talents will help the team consider all the possibilities and make the most productive and effective decisions about your church's future.

☐ If you also have exceptional talent in themes such as Developer or Individualization, you may be a good spiritual mentor to those new to the faith. Your Strategic talents will help them see the best opportunities for growth and service, and you will grow by helping someone else grow.

☐ Jesus said, "So do not worry about tomorrow, for tomorrow will bring worries of its own" (Matthew 6:34a). Armed with your Strategic talents, you are quick to determine the best course of action in any situation. Live at peace knowing that no matter what comes tomorrow, your God-given talents will be there to get you through.

☐ Trust your intuitive insights as often as possible. Even though you might not be able to explain them rationally, your intuitions are created by a brain that instinctively anticipates and forecasts. Have confidence in these intuitions.

☐ Musing time is essential to strategic thinking. Take the time to fully reflect or muse about a goal that your congregation wants to achieve until the related patterns and issues emerge for you. Then share your insights with your congregation's leaders.

☐ Talk with your pastor about the alternative directions you see that could help accomplish the church's mission. Detailed conversations like this can be a great asset in your church's planning processes, and they can help you become even better at anticipating possible outcomes.

WOO

If you are particularly talented in Woo, you love the challenge of meeting new people and winning them over. You derive satisfaction from breaking the ice and making a connection with another person.

☐ Join a church study or social group of people you do not know yet. You'll enjoy the excitement of meeting new people.

☐ Be a greeter at worship services. Your Woo talents will help people feel welcome.

☐ Offer to welcome and sponsor new members. You can quickly connect with people, put them at ease, and help them feel comfortable.

☐ Be a builder of goodwill for your church by getting to know the people who live near you. Reach out to your community. Offer to welcome new people and invite them to serve.

☐ Ask others thought-provoking questions, such as "What is the most meaningful religious experience you've had?" and engage in uplifting conversations that will help you feel connected to God in daily life.

☐ Take charge of a large social event such as a church fundraising auction or dinner. Use your charm to create positive feelings.

☐ Learn the names of as many church members as you can. Build a card file of the people you know, and add names as you become acquainted. Include a snippet of personal information — such as their birthday, favorite color, hobby, or other personal interest.

☐ You are a natural campaigner. Is there an important project or ministry in your church that needs a broad base of support to succeed? Use your Woo talents to bring others on board and turn a dream into reality.

☐ In group settings, take responsibility for helping put new or more reserved people at ease. Your Woo talents can help others experience your church as warm, inviting, and accepting.

☐ Be ready to find the right words to explain that your affinity for networking is one of your gifts. If you don't explain your Woo talents, others might mistake them for insincerity and wonder why you are being so friendly.

CHAPTER 4

Helping Others
Find the Right Fit

Whether you are a pastor, church staff member, or lay leader, surely you collaborate with other people to accomplish the mission of your church. Understanding your talents and strengths, and those of the people you work with, can dramatically improve your effectiveness and accomplishments.

When you understand the strengths approach and put it into practice, you realize that capitalizing on what you and those around you naturally do best is so much more productive than trying to "fix" yourselves.

It took Bonnie a couple of tries before she found a role in her church that was right for her. She was fairly new to her church and wanted to get involved. So one Sunday, she answered a plea from the Christian education director to be a youth group sponsor. "I thought, 'How hard can that be?' I was young (or so I thought). I had been a teenager once, so I thought I could relate to them," she remembers.

Bonnie was wrong. "It was a disaster," she says. "The lessons were frustrating. I couldn't relate to the kids. Their questions always caught me off guard and I felt stupid. Fortunately — for me and the kids — I was able to get out of it, and they found a much better sponsor." Bonnie then tried ushering and discovered she wasn't very good at that, either. She didn't have a knack for thinking on her feet or for meeting new people.

But one day Bonnie noticed that the church grounds needed "sprucing up" with some flowerbeds. She says, "I summoned my courage and went to the trustees and asked if I could do that — and to my surprise they said, 'Go for it!' So I got to plan the flower arrangements — the types and colors, the location, all of that. I'm really into detail and order, and I seem to have a knack for putting together patterns of colors. And I just love to garden. It was a perfect fit, and I couldn't be happier."

It's a good thing Bonnie was persistent. Others might have just given up after experiencing only one disappointing "wrong fit."

MANAGING LESSER TALENTS

Truly successful and fulfilled people like Bonnie know the deep truth of this maxim: *You will be successful because of who you are, not because of who you are not.* How can you help people do what they naturally do best rather than try to "fix" them? How can you position people in your congregation so that they can

182

develop strengths while furthering the mission of your church? You'll find the answers in the following four proven management tactics.

Whenever possible, avoid using your areas of lesser talent. A lesser talent becomes a weakness *only when you try to use it*.

Lisa grew up in a small town and attended a very traditional church. "Sometimes in church, I felt a lot of pressure to do things that were just very foreign to me," she says. In the small-town church, there was an unspoken expectation that women were the ones who were supposed to volunteer to work in the nursery. "After all, it's taking care of kids, and women are supposed to be more nurturing, right? Well, that just wasn't me," Lisa remembers. "But now, at this church, there's no pressure to be something you're not, and so I decided to get involved in the music ministry. I discovered that I love to sing, and I'm not half bad, even though I've never sung in public before. It's refreshing not to feel like I have to do something I'm not good at."

Use support systems. The majority of adults in this country have one shortcoming in common, and we use a support system to manage this imperfection. The weakness is our eyesight. Every morning, millions of us wake up and immediately use a support system — our glasses or contact lenses — without giving it a second thought. If you are a pastor, when you get up to preach every Sunday, you most likely use a support system: a microphone to help your voice project so you can be heard.

There's a story about a prominent Protestant minister who was getting ready to lead the congregation in The Lord's Prayer. He stood up in the pulpit, faced his congregation of several hundred people, and began by saying, "Let us join together in the prayer our Lord taught us." He continued, "Now I lay me down to sleep, I pray the Lord my soul to keep." When he noticed that no one was praying, the pastor realized what he was saying and stopped in mid-sentence. He looked at his congregation for a second, and then, without a word, stepped down from the pulpit and walked off through the door at the side of the chancel into his nearby study.

The pastor sat down at his typewriter, opened his Bible to Christ's Sermon on the Mount, and tapped out the words to The Lord's Prayer. When he finished, he went right back into the pulpit and tacked the freshly typed words to the prayer right in the middle of the pulpit, where he would be sure to always see it.

As if nothing had happened, he started over, "Let us join together in the prayer our Lord taught us." And never again did he rely on memory when leading the congregation in The Lord's Prayer — he had a support system.

Establish complementary partnerships. When God spoke to Moses through the burning bush and called him to go back to Egypt to lead the Israelites to freedom, Moses was full of excuses about why he wasn't qualified. Moses told God, "I have never been eloquent, neither in the past nor even now that you have spoken to your servant; but I am slow of speech and slow of tongue" (Exodus 4:10). So God found Moses a partner — Moses' brother Aaron. Moses had the talent for leading and for devising strategy, but he couldn't wow a crowd with his oratory or stand before kings and summon the appropriate words. Aaron could. And together, Moses and Aaron made a great team — which got even stronger with the addition of their sister Miriam. Power struggles notwithstanding (see Numbers 12), this trio brought their individual talents and strengths together into a combination — a complementary partnership — that multiplied their effectiveness exponentially.

Examples of effective team building can be found in everyday life, too. Jay, the lay leader in his church, learned the same lessons that Moses did. "Chairing our church's strategic mapping team was one of the most rewarding experiences of my spiritual life," says Jay. His congregation was at a crossroads, and the pastor put together a team that was charged with rewriting the church's mission, vision, and values statement. The team members would also restructure the church's organizational plan to reflect the new statement, and they would propose major program changes to better carry out the church's mission.

"It was daunting," Jay recalls. "I still think the pastor had some divine intervention in choosing the team, because the combination of talents represented by the nine of us was perfect for the task." Some of those themes still stick out in Jay's mind. "I have Focus, Arranger, and Command in my Signature Themes, so I was able to keep us on track, juggle our responsibilities, and keep us moving toward action — as well as make some tough decisions when disagreements occurred."

Two members of Jay's team, Adam and John, had Futuristic and Strategic among their top themes, so they were able to paint the picture of what their church could be like 10 or 15 years down the road — and then sort out the options for getting there. Another team member, Amy, had exceptional Analytical talents, and she kept everyone asking the right questions. "She really made us do our homework to make sure we were on the right path," Jay says.

Of two other team members, Jay recalls, "Terry had great Belief talents that were so valuable in helping us assess our values, and Sonya's Positivity kept things fun — which was such a blessing when we were doing such important work. Our teamwork was a great success, and now — seven years later — our congregation is still relying on the work we did."

There is no denying the power of the right fit when building teams. The right combination of complementary talents produces powerful results.

Leverage your own talents and strengths. Another way to manage your weaknesses is to rely on your strengths to overcome your lesser talents. "I even surprised myself when I volunteered to work as a counselor in our crisis center," says Robert. "I mean, I'm not a 'touchy-feely, tell-me-all-your problems' kind of guy.

People tell me I can be pretty insensitive, and I guess that's true — a lot of times I'll hurt someone's feelings without even realizing it."

At first glance, the counseling role didn't seem like it would be a good match, but something inside kept urging Robert to do it. "I think it was God telling me to stretch myself," he says. "Anyway, I've always been interested in psychology, what makes people tick and stuff, and I really wanted to help."

So Robert jumped in and found out that he really enjoyed it — and his supervisor has given him a lot of positive feedback. "I'm able to listen to people's problems without getting emotionally involved and then help them sort out options in a nonjudgmental way," he says. "Of course, I'm smart enough to know when I'm in over my head and when to refer someone to a professional. But for a rank amateur, I think I do all right!"

Robert doesn't have much talent in Empathy, so he doesn't instinctively draw on that theme to help those who talk to him. But his talents in the Restorative and Strategic themes make up for this and enable him to be involved in a ministry he really is passionate about.

TALENTS, STRENGTHS, AND SPIRITUAL GIFTS

You may be wondering how discovering your talents and building and applying strengths fits in with the concept of Spiritual Gifts. Paul makes several references to Spiritual Gifts in his letters in the New Testament, and no two references are exactly alike:

We have gifts that differ according to the grace given to us: prophecy, in proportion to faith; ministry, in ministering; the teacher, in teaching; the exhorter, in exhortation; the giver, in generosity; the leader, in diligence; the compassionate, in cheerfulness.

Romans 12:6-8

Now there are varieties of gifts, but the same Spirit; and there are varieties of services, but the same Lord; and there are varieties of activities, but it is the same God who activates all of them in everyone. To each is given the manifestation of the Spirit for the common good. To one is given through the Spirit the utterance of wisdom, and to another the utterance of knowledge according to the same Spirit, to another faith by the same Spirit, to another gifts of healing by the one Spirit, to another the working of miracles, to another prophecy, to another the discernment of spirits, to another various kinds of tongues, to another the interpretation of tongues. All these are activated by one and the same Spirit, who allots to each one individually just as the Spirit chooses.

1 Corinthians 12:4-11

The gifts he gave were that some would be apostles, some prophets, some evangelists, some pastors and teachers, to equip the saints for the work of ministry, for building up the body of Christ.

Ephesians 4:11-12

We don't want to get into a discussion about the Spiritual Gifts of healing, miracle working, or speaking in tongues. That's not our area of expertise, and theologians and biblical scholars have debated the meaning of those Gifts for centuries. But if you look at the other Spiritual Gifts that Paul lists — teaching, evangelization, leadership, and such — you will see that these Gifts really describe functions of ministry within the Church.

These Spiritual Gifts, then, perhaps more accurately can be called ministry areas, or areas of calling. Paul does, however, make it clear that these Gifts are to be used for the betterment and advancement of the Church: "to equip the saints [members] for the work of ministry, for building up the body of Christ."

Through the centuries, Christians have sought to identify and put into practice their unique Spiritual Gifts or callings. Identifying your talents isn't intended to take the place of identifying your Spiritual Gifts, but rather, it can be a powerful way to enhance your Gifts and calling. Your Spiritual Gifts help you find *what* the ministry is that God wants to see you accomplish; your talents are God's way of showing you *how* you will accomplish it.

Ron and Gina understand this. Along with being members of the same congregation, they have much in common: Both believe they have the Spiritual Gift of evangelization; they both have a passion for sharing their faith so that others may discover the abundant life they have found as followers of Jesus Christ. However, their talents are somewhat different. Ron's Signature Themes include Communication, Woo, and Significance, while Gina's include Relator, Empathy, and Harmony.

"My involvement in prison ministry has been life changing, not to mention eye opening," says Ron. "I lead a Bible study there once a week, and it's a real challenge. A lot of times guys will show up just to do something — anything but sit around their cell. And they'll come in with this chip on their shoulder, like, 'You aren't going to reach me with this Jesus stuff.' And I make it my personal mission to reach guys like this, and I see their lives begin to change when they open up to God's love. It's such a rush for me to see them start to respond and know that I was the one God used to reach them." Ron's success in his Spiritual Gift of evangelization depends on his productive application of his natural talents.

So too with Gina, whose "heart just aches when I see my friends going through rough times." She says, "Those are the times when I feel God can use me to either revive or deepen someone's faith." Gina wants all her friends to know how much they can depend on God to see them through the tough times of their lives — that all they have to do is turn to God and God will be there. "Their lives would be so much more satisfying," she says, "and things would go so much smoother for them if they turn all their problems — their entire lives — over to God for His direction."

So if Gina knows someone well enough, she'll talk to them about what a difference her faith has meant to her. "It's really just being a friend, that's all," she concludes.

Both Ron and Gina are living out their Spiritual Gifts of evangelization. But the ways they do it — the steps they take to achieve their outcomes — are totally different. They are different because Ron and Gina have different talents.

If you have started the process of helping people in your church discover their Spiritual Gifts, then helping them do the same with their talents would provide a powerful combination. Identifying Spiritual Gifts defines the outcome; discovering talents defines the steps.

CHAPTER 5

Creating Strengths-Based Congregations

What would the Church (or an individual congregation, for that matter) look like if leaders and members embraced a strengths-based approach to ministry? What if every Christian was encouraged to actively develop and use his or her talents to strengthen the Body of Christ and further the mission of the Church universal? Just imagine!

But before we take off into the realm of those possibilities (a real treat for those of you with Ideation or Futuristic among your Signature Themes), let's first explore how the early witnesses to the faith described the Church. We'll see that those witnesses focused on individuals' talents and the development of strengths when organizing this fledgling community. Indeed, their approach two millennia ago — spelled out explicitly in the New Testament — is as relevant as ever today; the Church urgently needs a strengths-based revitalization.

Let's be honest: The modern Church — Protestant, Catholic, and Orthodox — is in trouble; most people don't find its message relevant. But it wasn't always that way. In the beginning, the Church was bold and transformational. People's lives were changed by the message of salvation and by belonging to a community in which dramatic change was the norm. Finding salvation in Jesus Christ encouraged people — set them free, really — to focus on being the unique individuals God created them to be. And by living in community with others who had discovered this truth, they found opportunities to "build each other up" — to encourage one another to discover their talents, build strengths, and maximize their gifts.

Early leaders of the Church truly believed that Jesus' life, death, and resurrection had ushered in a "new Creation," or at least the realization of God's original intent of Creation. They believed that they were living at the beginning of the time when God was "making all things new" (Revelation 21:5). This created a sense of excitement, of urgency, in everything they did. They invited friends, neighbors, family members, and even strangers to "come and see" the new thing that God was doing in their midst. They wanted others to experience the new life they had found in Jesus and to know the fulfillment they had found living out this new life with others who had experienced it.

There was, to be sure, a missionary zeal among the leaders of the early Church. Luke's account of the birth of the Church — in the New Testament's Acts of the Apostles — is replete with stories of the early leaders' missionary journeys. Peter and the rest of the disciples, and Paul and his partners Barnabas, Silas, Timothy, and others, all traveled outside the bounds of Judea to spread the Gospel (the story of Jesus' life, death, and resurrection) and what it meant to have "new life in Christ." Early believers were encouraged to find their place in the new community and to discover their gifts in order to be truly fulfilled as followers of Jesus.

To better understand how the early Church transformed not only individual lives, but also the social fabric of first-century Palestine, let's dig deeper into three key New Testament passages. Within these passages — Acts 2:43-47, Acts 6:1-7, and 1 Corinthians 12:12-27 — are clues to building a strengths-based congregation and Church.

The evangelist Luke was a key witness to the power of the early Church, and he wrote about this power in his Gospel and in Acts; together, the Gospel of Luke and the Acts of the Apostles make up one-quarter of the New Testament. In the second chapter of Acts, Luke gives us an important insight into the essence of the early Church:

Awe came upon everyone, because many wonders and signs were being done by the apostles. All who believed were together and had all things in common; they would sell their possessions and goods and distribute the proceeds to all, as any had need. Day by day, as they spent much time together in the temple, they broke bread at home and ate their food with glad and generous hearts, praising God and having the goodwill of all the people. And day by day the Lord added to their number those who were being saved.
Acts 2:43-47

In these five verses, Luke describes what it meant to live in response to the good news of Jesus' life, death, and resurrection: Unity in spirit and in life, care for the poor, and the worship and praise of God. Let's look at these points a bit more closely.

The early Church lived out unity in spirit and in life. Even the casual reader of this passage from Acts will notice that the unity Luke stressed was a hallmark of the early Church; its members "had all things in common." The Church broke down the social barriers that were entrenched in the first-century Roman Empire. Unlike life in Roman society, in the Church, the poor interacted with the rich, the uneducated with the educated, the men with the women — and all were considered equal.

What mattered was not wealth or social position or gender, but a belief in Jesus Christ and the talents, strengths, and gifts that individuals could bring to and develop in the new community. In the early Church, people were valued for who God created them to be, not for the role they were forced to conform to in Roman society.

The early Church cared for the poor. In this instance and others, Luke described a community in which the needs of the poor were addressed. In some instances, the members of a congregation shared their possessions with the poor. In other instances, individual members of a congregation kept their possessions but gave liberally of what they had so that the poor were supported.

The important thing to note is that, in a rigidly stratified society in which wealth and poverty were seen as divine reward and punishment, the Church went against the cultural norm and said that individuals matter. Because individuals were uniquely created by God and reconciled to God through Jesus Christ, the members of the Church had a responsibility to ensure that everyone's basic needs were met.

196

After all, how were individuals going to develop strengths, make the most of their gifts, and fulfill God's purposes for their lives when they were in need of such basics as food, clothing, and shelter?

The early Church praised God. The leaders of the early Church never forgot that God was the source of all they were and all they had. They were not "self-made" by any means; most of the original leaders were Jesus' disciples, and most of them were peasants. They were ordinary people with no designs on greatness.

But they realized that they were called by God to proclaim the good news of God's love for humanity — a love poured out in the life, death, and resurrection of Jesus Christ. Each of them had talents, and God used those unique talents to start a movement — through these ordinary people — that would change the world. The early Church kept its focus on the source of strength and new life and hope, never passing up an opportunity to praise and worship God.

THE EXPONENTIAL POWER OF DELEGATION

Due to the enthusiasm and authenticity of this diverse group of believers, the Church grew quickly. The appeal of the message, the promise of new life, and the acceptance and celebration of individual uniqueness formed a powerful combination that made this new movement an irresistible force. But the rapid growth created a problem: The original leaders, the apostles, couldn't do everything themselves. They needed help.

Indeed, the apostles were confronted with a valid complaint: Some of the widows were not getting their daily allotment of food. This was a critical concern because in first-century culture, widows were among the most vulnerable members of society. In a time when a single woman earned little, if anything, widows were dependent on the kindness of others. The early Church made a commitment to care for the "least of these," just as Jesus had taught them. As a result, the leaders felt it was their obligation as followers of Christ to ensure that the poor and the destitute were cared for. And, the vast majority of widows fell into this category. So when the apostles learned that some of the widows weren't being fed, it was cause for alarm.

But they were in a bind. The apostles were the primary leaders of the new movement, and most of their time and energy was spent casting the vision, preaching and teaching, and seeing to the spiritual growth and health of the community. What's more, their talents, gifts, and callings were to leadership. Looking after the widows required *management.*

At first, the apostles tried to lead *and* manage — which is how they found themselves in this predicament in the first place. The solution they devised was elegant in its simplicity and brilliant in its clarity: Why not find others who have the talents, gifts, and calling for administration?

Now during those days, when the disciples were increasing in number, the Hellenists complained against the Hebrews because their widows were being neglected in the daily distribution of food. And the twelve called together the whole community of the disciples and said, "It is not right that we should neglect the word of God to wait on tables. Therefore, friends, select from among yourselves seven men of good standing, full of the Spirit and of wisdom, whom we may appoint to this task, while we, for our part, will devote ourselves to prayer and to serving the word." What they said pleased the whole community, and they chose Stephen, a man full of faith and the Holy Spirit, together with Philip, Prochorus, Nicanor, Timon, Parmenas, and Nicolaus, a proselyte of Antioch. They had these men stand before the apostles, who prayed and laid their hands on them.

The word of God continued to spread; the number of the disciples increased greatly in Jerusalem, and a great many of the priests became obedient to the faith.

Acts 6:1-7

Clearly, when people serve in roles that fit their talents and gifts, God does marvelous things.

PAUL'S WISDOM AND MINISTRY

The book of Acts isn't the only place in the New Testament where we find clues about how strongly the leaders of the early Church felt about the uniqueness of individuals — a uniqueness created by, blessed by, and encouraged by God. In Acts, Luke tells us about one of the greatest leaders of the early church: the apostle Paul. We also have Paul's own words in the New Testament. As a leader of the Church, Paul wrote letters of instruction to churches he founded — and several of those letters are contained in the New Testament.

199

Paul was born "Saul" in the ancient Near Eastern city of Tarsus (in what is now present-day Turkey), a Jew by birth who was also a Roman citizen. As an adult, he became a Pharisee, a recognized expert on Jewish religious law. By Luke's account and by Paul's own admission, Paul persecuted the members of the early Church. And according to Luke in Acts 7-8, Paul (Saul) was present at the stoning of the first Christian martyr, Stephen.

Acts 9 recounts Paul's dramatic conversion to Christianity on the road to Damascus, where he encountered the risen Christ and was confronted with his persecution of the Church. After his conversion, Paul traveled throughout the Mediterranean, founding several churches in the major cities of the area. And when he finally reached Rome, he died as a martyr to the faith he once set out to destroy.

Paul's letters offer a fascinating and important glimpse into the inner life of the early Church. They also provide insight into the most powerful theological mind of the first century. For our purposes, we've chosen to focus on a profound idea that Paul shared with the Church at Corinth. In the twelfth chapter of his first letter to the Corinthians, Paul explains how each member of the Church is part of the Body of Christ, and just as the different members of the physical body have different functions, so too do the members of the spiritual Body of Christ:

For just as the body is one and has many members, and all the members of the body, though many, are one body, so it is with Christ. For in the one Spirit we were all baptized into one body

— Jews or Greeks, slaves or free — and we were all made to drink of one Spirit.

Indeed, the body does not consist of one member but of many. If the foot would say, "Because I am not a hand, I do not belong to the body," that would not make it any less a part of the body. And if the ear would say, "Because I am not an eye, I do not belong to the body," that would not make it any less a part of the body. If the whole body were an eye, where would the hearing be? If the whole body were hearing, where would the sense of smell be? But as it is, God arranged the members in the body, each one of them, as he chose. If all were a single member, where would the body be? As it is, there are many members, yet one body. The eye cannot say to the hand, "I have no need of you," nor again the head to the feet, "I have no need of you." On the contrary, the members of the body that seem to be weaker are indispensable, and those members of the body that we think less honorable we clothe with greater honor, and our less respectable members are treated with greater respect; whereas our more respectable members do not need this. But God has so arranged the body, giving the greater honor to the inferior member, that there may be no dissension within the body, but the members may have the same care for one another. If one member suffers, all suffer together with it; if one member is honored, all rejoice together with it.

Now you are the body of Christ and individually members of it.

1 Corinthians 12:12-27

If the Church was to be true to the purpose for which God intended it, Paul asserted, then individual talents and gifts needed to be not only recognized, but celebrated. If we look more closely at these verses, we'll see that Paul is essentially advocating a strengths-based congregation.

Unity in Christ. This letter to the Corinthians, like all the other letters in the New Testament, was not written in a vacuum. Paul was addressing some specific problems that had arisen in the young Corinthian Church. There were some in the Church at Corinth who believed that some talents and Spiritual Gifts were more valuable than others, and that members who had these "special gifts" were more important than other members of the congregation.

Paul wrote to correct that misguided notion, and he began by reminding the Corinthians that all gifts come from the Holy Spirit and that all members of the Church are one in Jesus Christ. Neither birthright ("Jews or Greeks") nor social position ("slaves or free") makes any difference; we "were all baptized into one body" and "made to drink of one Spirit." If a church is truly to become a strengths-based congregation, it must never forget that its foundation rests upon unity with all other Christians in Jesus Christ.

Diversity of talents and gifts. After establishing that the foundation of the Church is unity in Christ, Paul launched into his brilliant comparison of the metaphorical "Body of Christ" to an actual human body. Just as the human body is made up of many parts, so too is the Body of Christ. The entire human body isn't an ear or a hand or a foot or an eye, but rather is made up of many parts, each with different functions.

Paul said it is like that in the Church — the Body of Christ — as well; the Church isn't made up entirely of prophets or teachers or counselors or administrators. There is a diversity of talent in the Church just as there is a diversity of functions of the parts of the human body.

And members of the Body of Christ shouldn't all strive to have the same talent or gift, just as ears shouldn't strive to be eyes or hands strive to be feet.

The whole is greater than the sum of its parts. The human body is a marvel to behold. When it is functioning properly, the ears hear, the eyes see, the feet walk, the heart pumps blood — all the parts work together in harmony. But when one part of your body isn't working properly, perhaps due to injury or illness, it affects everything else. If you've ever experienced the truth of the adage, "When your feet hurt, you hurt all over," you can better understand Paul's words: "If one member suffers, all suffer together with it; if one member is honored, all rejoice together with it."

Paul's illustration points to an important truth: *We need each other.* Together, as the Body of Christ, we can accomplish so much more than we ever could alone. When we recognize, celebrate, and develop the diversity of talents that live among us, we are fulfilling God's purpose not just for our individual lives, but also for the Church.

THE STRENGTHS-BASED CONGREGATION IN THE 21ST CENTURY

The idea of the strengths-based congregation, with its roots in the early Church, is not relegated solely to the first century. There are living, breathing examples of strengths-based congregations flourishing today. Stories about people whose lives have changed have been pouring out from these churches. We'd like to share some of these stories.

Bill, a pastor in a mid-sized parish in New York, discovered the amazing power of focusing on strengths when his study group decided to get together after a summer break. The group really hadn't jelled, and Bill was looking for a way to help the members really become a "group," not just individuals who occasionally get together. Bill suggested that they share a Clifton StrengthsFinder experience. "Everyone was up for it," Bill says, "including some who hadn't been showing up at all."

Eleven group members participated, with one member acting as the facilitator. "In the first week," Bill reports, "everyone got their books, and the facilitator led us through some activities that helped us gain a better perspective on the whole idea of discovering talents and building strengths. By the second week, we all went online to take the Clifton StrengthsFinder, and each one, to a person, found it to be uncannily accurate. Good discussion followed."

Bill says, "But the third session broke the bank at Monte Carlo! We formed groups that were designated by our Signature Themes, and we shared how we've helped people by using our talents and strengths. As we did this, there was a growing openness and ease among the group members, almost like time-lapse photography. You could actually see and feel a level of freedom and engagement taking place right before your eyes. It was noticeably more relaxed and more intense than anything we had experienced in three years of meeting."

They formally ended the session and gathered for some refreshments. Bill says, "No joke, the conversation that spontaneously followed was mind-blowing! Each person was speaking about his or her faith experiences to a degree that was at once relaxed and unbelievable. One man even turned to his wife and said, 'I don't think I ever told you this dear, but . . .' One story of spiritual experience and commitment led to another, and all of a sudden, it was 20 minutes to midnight, and no one noticed the time passing."

There was no doubt in the group members' minds that going through the strengths exercises for three weeks inspired them to share their faith in a way that they hadn't in three years. "In fact," Bill says, "it was fascinating to hear people comment on the stories by pointing out each other's talents and strengths in action. Amazing! Everyone had heartfelt expressions of gratitude for being able to share their deepest faith experiences with others who didn't think they were nuts, but quite genuine.

"These are the tools" Bill continues, "to get the Church back on track, to turn over the soil, to get rid of the thorns and weeds, and to be able to produce a hundredfold from the seed God has already sown. Discovering our talents has definitely been a tipping point!"

In fact, discovering talents and building strengths has implications beyond your church. Knowing and living your greatest talents is a powerful way to positively influence others' lives. Consider the story of one of Bill's parishioners, Mike, who is a member of the church council and actively involved in various other ministries. Last year, the

205

small Bible study group Mike belonged to decided to focus on discovering their talents, and each member took the Clifton StrengthsFinder assessment. Mike learned that among his five Signature Themes were Maximizer, Arranger, and Relator — themes of talent that he could readily see at work in his life.

Mike had worked for 15 years at the local Honda dealership, starting right out of high school and working his way up to become the manager of the parts department. His department was arranged for maximum efficiency. When his mechanics needed a part, he always knew where the part was, and he never let his inventory run low on any part. He had invested time and energy in maximizing his mechanics' productivity, and he took pride in seeing to it that they had everything they needed to be successful in their jobs. His top themes made him successful and appreciated at the Honda dealership — until it was sold.

The new owners weren't concerned about relationships with customers or employees — relationships that had made the dealership successful over the years. Consequently, many long-time employees left for other jobs. One day, a former employee, who had landed a job at a larger Honda dealership in a different part of the city, called Mike to tell him about an opening for a parts department manager. Mike decided to apply for the position, and in the interview, the owner asked Mike what he thought his strengths were. Mike replied, "I not only think I know what my strengths are, I actually know my top five themes of talent." Mike described each of his Signature Themes and how they help him succeed in work and life.

"Where did you learn this?" asked the astonished owner.

"In my church group," replied Mike.

"No kidding?" remarked the owner. "You mean you actually learned something useful at church?" Mike got the job, and the owner started attending Mike's church.

One day, Bill stopped by the dealership to see how Mike's new job was going. "Like the Maximizer and Arranger he is, Mike had the parts department organized and humming along at maximum efficiency," Bill says. "But the really remarkable thing was the look on the mechanics' faces when they came to Mike with parts needs and questions." They were happy, relaxed, and seemed to truly enjoy Mike's presence. Bill asked one of the mechanics about it, and he said, "Before Mike came, all the mechanics were ready to quit. They were so frustrated by the disorganization in the parts department and the shabby way the parts manager treated them." But when Mike came on board, there was a huge change in attitude and performance — and the mechanics stayed. Mike was able to bring out the best in them because he was living through his greatest talents and the strengths he had built upon them.

As Mike's story illustrates, we take our talents and strengths with us wherever we go, and the positive effects benefit not only ourselves and our fellow congregation members, but also our family, our friends, and our coworkers. Discovering talent and building strengths is also a way for those who are already engaged in their congregation to find a better fit for themselves. Janice's story is a case in point.

Janice was always active in her church, a large Protestant congregation in the Midwest. In fact, her pastor says that she is one of those people who can sometimes get too busy. Among other things, Janice had created her church's women's Bible study program from scratch. She developed the topics, found the curriculum, coordinated teachers, and in general, created a growing, thriving Bible study program that is the "crown jewel" of the women's ministry in her church. But after accomplishing all this, she was starting to feel somewhat empty — even a bit restless.

When her pastor offered a class on strengths, Janice signed up and discovered her five Signature Themes. As she learned about her talents, she realized why she was feeling restless. Achiever and Maximizer are two of her top themes, so maintaining a ministry at its current level — even if that level is excellence — isn't going to fulfill her. As an Achiever, she needs to feel like she's accomplishing something, moving forward. And her Maximizer talents drive that momentum toward excellence. She realized that she felt like she had accomplished all she could with the women's Bible study program, and maintaining the program at its current level was not going to be satisfying. She needed a new challenge. She needed something she could work hard at developing and taking to excellence.

After several discussions with her pastor and the leader of the women's ministry, Janice is now developing a church-wide program to focus on talent discovery and strengths development (which plays right into her Maximizer theme). It's a lot of hard work, but Janice once again feels personally fulfilled and spiritually nourished — because she is in a ministry that helps her maximize her talents.

EVERYONE NEEDS A COACH

One of the keys to Janice's success was that she had a "coach" — someone in her congregation who talked to her one-on-one about her talents. Janice's coach gave her valuable feedback on her talents and showed her how her talents are at work in her life (and come as naturally as breathing). Because of this, Janice began to see ministry opportunities in which she could be successful because of those talents.

If we accept the fact that our Signature Themes are the primary lenses through which we see the world, then we also must accept that we are in many ways blind to our own talents. We need others to help us see our talents and strengths and help us develop them to their full potential. As Proverbs 27:17 states, "As iron sharpens iron, so one man sharpens another" (NIV). A trusted advisor who acts as a coach can help "sharpen our edges" and help us fulfill our potential.

Rhonda's experience with a coach changed both her marriage and her ministry. Because she was new to her church, taking the Clifton StrengthsFinder was a quick way to plant her feet firmly within the congregation. After just a one-hour "coaching session," Rhonda was able to walk away with a new understanding and perspective on her marriage (both she and her husband, Dave, had taken the Clifton StrengthsFinder). By learning their Signature Themes, Rhonda and Dave learned more about each other and why they acted and thought the way they did. The Clifton StrengthsFinder opened up a whole new path of communication for them and gave them a new language to describe why and how they act the way they do.

Rhonda also discovered a ministry area in her church that fit her talents. With exceptional talent in themes like Discipline, Relator, Communication, Activator, and Command (and the Spiritual Gifts of Exhorting and Encouraging), along with a passion for writing, Rhonda quickly agreed to be a part of the creative writing ministry at the church. Her first writing assignment was to encourage the rest of the congregation by sharing her own story of how God had affected her marriage and family.

A good coach can help people see talents and strengths that they often cannot see for themselves. Chris, who has had a great deal of experience coaching others in her church, was helping her friend Angie discover how to best apply talents from her Signature Themes to her life and work.

Chris says that Angie was able to see how her talents applied to her work at the office. However, understanding how she was using them in her family life was not as clear. One morning, they were sitting in Angie's kitchen discussing her talents. In the middle of their conversation, the phone rang. A family member had just died, and funeral arrangements were in progress. "From the sound of things," says Chris, "some family members were upset and unsure how best to handle everything. But Angie knew just the right things to say and do. I started jotting down notes about the conversation, and when Angie hung up the phone, I handed her my notes — notes that related the phone conversation I overheard to her Signature Themes: Harmony, Arranger, Empathy, Context, and Restorative."

As Angie looked at Chris' notes, she started to see the relationship. "I began to connect the dots," says Angie. "I understood how my areas of talent guided my interaction with my family members." Angie's talents helped calm the waters of a crisis.

TALENTS: MAKE THE MOST OF THEM

Before we close this chapter, we want to examine one more New Testament text — a text that is perhaps more relevant than any other concerning talents, strengths, and gifts and the importance of using them wisely. According to the Gospel of Matthew, the following is one of the last parables Jesus told his disciples before his passion, death, and resurrection:

[Jesus said]: "For it is as if a man, going on a journey, summoned his slaves and entrusted his property to them; to one he gave five talents,* to another two, to another one, to each according to his ability. Then he went away. The one who had

received the five talents went off at once and traded with them, and made five more talents. In the same way, the one who had the two talents made two more talents. But the one who had received the one talent went off and dug a hole in the ground and hid his master's money. After a long time the master of those slaves came and settled accounts with them. Then the one who had received the five talents came forward, bringing five more talents, saying, 'Master, you handed over to me five talents; see, I have made five more talents.' His master said to him, 'Well done, good and trustworthy slave; you have been trustworthy in a few things, I will put you in charge of many things; enter into the joy of your master.' And the one with the two talents also came forward, saying, 'Master, you handed over to me two talents; see, I have made two more talents.' His master said to him, 'Well done, good and trustworthy slave; you have been trustworthy in a few things, I will put you in charge of many things; enter into the joy of your master.' Then the one who had received the one talent also came forward, saying, 'Master, I knew that you were a harsh man, reaping where you did not sow, and gathering where you did not scatter seed; so I was afraid, and I went and hid your talent in the ground. Here you have what is yours.' But his master replied, 'You wicked and lazy slave! You knew, did you, that I reap where I did not sow, and gather where I did not scatter? Then you ought to have invested my money with the bankers, and on my return I would have received what was my own with interest. So take the talent from him, and give it to the one with the ten talents. For to all those who have, more will be given, and they will have an abundance; but from those who have nothing, even what they have will be taken away.'"

Matthew 25:14-29

We find it significant, of course, that the word for the amount of money Jesus was talking about in the parable — talent — is the same word we use for "a pattern of thought, feeling, or behavior that can be productively applied." The point of Jesus' parable wasn't about investing huge sums of money (the amount of money given to the slave who received five talents would be worth about one million dollars today!), but rather it was about using the talents that God places within each one of us. God expects us to develop those talents and use them wisely.

Notice that not every slave was given the same amount of "talents"; each was given, said Jesus, "according to his ability." So it is with God and the distribution of talents and gifts among individuals. Our co-author, Don Clifton, was always fond of saying that each person can do something better than 10,000 other people. The key is for individuals to discover what that something is, and then do it.

In this parable, Jesus is expressing the same idea about God. The master gave each slave a sum of money that he expected the slaves to invest on his behalf while he was away. Then, upon his return, the master asked for an account of what each slave did with the money. The slaves who received five talents and two talents doubled their investment, and the master was pleased. The slave who received one talent did nothing with his, and the master was far from pleased; in fact, he was furious. Notice that the "one-talent" slave didn't lose the money. He kept it safe, thinking that his master would be pleased to just get back what was his. But the master had the opposite reaction; he wanted the slave to take a risk and grow his talent.

Indeed, developing our talents into strengths requires risk. We must step out, try new things, or take a chance by doing something we may fail at — at first. But if we do not take some risks — emotionally, physically, and spiritually — we will never grow.

God expects no less from us and from the Church.

CHAPTER 6

Discovering a Calling

When we think of a "calling," we usually imagine the voice of God coming in the night. We also think that people who are called are somehow special — unusually devout — and not "regular folks" like us. Our view is reflected in the call of Samuel, found in the Old Testament:

> *Now the boy Samuel was ministering to the LORD under Eli. The word of the LORD was rare in those days; visions were not widespread.*
>
> *At that time Eli, whose eyesight had begun to grow dim so that he could not see, was lying down in his room; the lamp of God had not yet gone out, and Samuel was lying down in the temple of the LORD, where the ark of God was. Then the LORD called, "Samuel! Samuel!" and he said, "Here I am!" and ran to Eli, and said, "Here I am, for you called me." But he said, "I did not call; lie down again." So he went and lay down.*
> 1 Samuel 3:1-5

Notice that Samuel didn't recognize the voice of God at first — he thought it was his mentor, Eli. But after three times (and some coaching from Eli), Samuel did recognize God's voice, responded to that call, and went on to become one of Israel's greatest prophets.

But callings aren't just for the devout and holy. Everyone has a calling. You just need to discover what it is. And that calling doesn't come from God's voice thundering from above; it comes from His whispers deep within you, from the very essence of your being. God expects nothing more from you than to live that life for which you were created. *He wants you to be yourself.*

When you discover your talents, you begin to discover your calling. When you develop your talents into strengths and apply those strengths, you fulfill your calling. Now, what do you think your calling might be? Take some time to reflect on the following:

- Dare to dream. If time and money were no object, what would you do for God?
- Where is your passion? What do you love to do?
- What are your greatest talents? How could you combine your talents and your passions to fulfill your calling?
- Talk to your pastor, your small group leader, or someone in your church who understands strengths-based organizations. Make a plan to explore the possibilities of combining your talents and your passions to fulfill your calling. It doesn't have to be in the church;

individuals' callings may lead them to such ministries as Habitat for Humanity, adult literacy projects, medical clinics for the poor, or Meals on Wheels — the possibilities are limitless. So are society's needs.

THE POWER OF BEING CALLED

Throughout the Bible, we see how people were called according to their talents to further God's vision for humankind. There was Abraham, who at the age of 75 had the courage to trust God and leave everything he had ever known to go to a place he had never seen. Relying on his talent for envisioning the future that God had promised him, he strategically forged alliances with foreign rulers to make his way as he lived in the new land.

There was Deborah, one of the judges of ancient Israel, who commanded respect and loyalty from the generals of the Israelite army. Her positivity inspired confidence in her followers in the face of overwhelming odds, and the song she sang of God's deliverance (one of the oldest portions of the Old Testament) celebrated her people's victory.

In the New Testament, when Jesus was first beginning his ministry, he walked by the Sea of Galilee and called his disciples. Each of them was uniquely created; each had a unique combination of talents. They were fishermen, government workers, businessmen, and students — "regular folks" like us.

Ever the activator, Peter was impetuous, ready to jump in without thinking things completely through — a man of action totally devoted to Jesus. Yet even when he made the greatest mistake of his life (denying that he ever knew Jesus), he recovered, found forgiveness, and tapped into those qualities that Jesus first saw in him — and became the leader of the new faith.

Thomas was cautious, analytical, always raising questions. And once he got the answers, he made known the strength of his conviction. Even when his demand for evidence of the Resurrection earned him the nickname "doubting Thomas," once he had his proof, he went on to eventually die for the Lord he loved.

Andrew was a fisherman, and after he was called, he was always looking for people to bring to Jesus so they, too, could have their lives changed. Andrew's talent for winning others over, his Woo, caused him to introduce his brother to Jesus — his brother Peter.

In so many ways, you are no different from the ordinary people with extraordinary talents who populate the Bible. Just like them, you too can find your calling. When you discover your talents and link those talents with your passion, there is no telling what God can accomplish through you.

God has created the one and only you, uniquely gifted with undeniable talents that are the foundation for your strengths.

Claim who you are, listen to God, celebrate your talents, begin living through strengths. And start transforming your life — and the life of your congregation.

A Technical Report on the Clifton StrengthsFinder:

What research underpins the Clifton StrengthsFinder, and what ongoing research is planned?

THE GALLUP ORGANIZATION
April 2004

FOREWORD

Many technical issues must be considered in the evaluation of an instrument such as the Clifton StrengthsFinder. One set of issues revolves around information technology and the expanding possibilities that Web-based applications offer for those who study human nature. Another set of issues involves what is known as psychometrics, which is the scientific study of human behavior through measurement. The Clifton StrengthsFinder is required to meet many American and international standards for psychometrics applied to test development (such as AERA/APA/NCME, 1999). The Clifton StrengthsFinder Technical Report deals with some questions that emerge from those standards as well as technical questions that a leader may have about the use of the Clifton StrengthsFinder in his or her organization.

A few technical references have been cited for readers who wish to review primary source material. These technical materials may be found in local university libraries or on the Internet. The reader is encouraged to review the sources cited at the end of the report and/or contact Gallup for further discussion.

WHAT IS THE CLIFTON STRENGTHSFINDER?

The Clifton StrengthsFinder is a Web-based talent assessment instrument from the perspective of Positive Psychology. Through a secure connection, the Clifton StrengthsFinder presents 180 items to the user. Each item lists a pair of potential self-descriptors, such as "I read instructions carefully" and "I like to jump right into things." The descriptors are placed as if anchoring polar ends of a continuum. From each pair, the participant is then asked to choose the descriptor that best describes him or her, and also the extent to which it does so. The participant is given 20 seconds to respond to a given item before the system moves on to the next item. (Clifton StrengthsFinder developmental research showed that the 20-second limit resulted in a negligible item noncompletion rate.)

WHAT IS POSITIVE PSYCHOLOGY?

For more than 50 years following World War II, psychology focused primarily on a pathology model, attempting to diagnose and treat mental illness. Research focused on repairing damage within a disease model of human functioning. Although this period yielded many important breakthroughs in the treatment of mental illness, psychology's predominant focus on the pathology model allowed for very little attention on the study of fulfilled individuals and thriving organizations.

223

A search of more than 100 years of the psychology literature found approximately 8,000 articles on anger, 58,000 on anxiety, and 71,000 on depression, while only about 850 articles on joy, 3,000 on happiness, and 5,700 on life satisfaction turned up. Articles on negative emotions surpassed those on positive emotions by a 14-1 ratio (Myers 2000).

A new perspective in psychology, led by such pioneers as Donald O. Clifton, Ph.D., and Martin Seligman, Ph.D., is known as Positive Psychology. Positive Psychology is defined as "the scientific study of optimal human functioning. It aims to discover and promote the factors that allow individuals and communities to thrive" (Sheldon, Fredrickson, Rathunde, & Csikszentmihalyi, 2000). Positive Psychology is about identifying the strengths in individuals and organizations, and helping them develop and excel based on these strengths. This new paradigm explores ways to help people flourish rather than simply function. Topics receiving attention within the Positive Psychology movement include courage, strength, wisdom, spirituality, happiness, hope, resiliency, confidence, satisfaction, and other related areas of study. These topics are studied at the individual level or in a work group, family, or community. The strong reception to this positive approach to psychology is evidenced through special journal issues devoted to Positive Psychology in the American Psychologist (January 2000, March 2001) and the Journal of Humanistic Psychology (Winter 2001), as well as a host of edited books on topics in the field of Positive

Psychology (Cameron, Dutton, & Quinn, 2003; Keyes & Haidt, 2003; Linley & Joseph, 2004; Lopez & Snyder, 2003; Snyder & Lopez, 2002).

The Gallup Organization has been a prominent and recognized leader in the Positive Psychology movement since inception. In January 2003, Dr. Clifton was awarded an American Psychological Association presidential commendation in recognition of his pioneering role in strengths-based psychology. The commendation states, "Whereas, living out the vision that life and work could be about building what is best and highest, not just about correcting weaknesses, [Clifton] became the father of Strengths-Based Psychology and the grandfather of Positive Psychology."

Gallup has sponsored and hosted the first five major Positive Psychology Summits, now attended annually by more than 300 research leaders, graduate students, and practitioners. Gallup is also actively involved in the science of Positive Psychology through theory development and empirical research in the areas of talent-based hiring, strengths-based development, employee engagement, and customer engagement. Further, many of the leading academics in the Positive Psychology field are members of Gallup's Senior Scientist program designed for global research leaders who teach at conferences and client programs, conduct publishable research, and lend their expertise to Gallup research design and consulting. Current Gallup Senior Scientists engaged in Positive Psychology research and instruction include Chip Anderson (Azusa Pacific University), Bruce Avolio (University of Nebraska-Lincoln), Mihaly Csikszentmihalyi (Claremont Graduate University), Ed Diener (University of Illinois-Urbana Champaign), Barbara Fredrickson (University of Michigan), Daniel Kahneman (Princeton University), Fred Luthans (University of Nebraska-Lincoln), and Phil Stone (Harvard University).

James K. Clifton, Gallup Chairman and CEO, articulated the following vision for the future of Positive Psychology in his letter to attendees of the First International Positive Psychology Summit.

> We believe many of the answers and solutions the world needs most lie within this new science [of Positive Psychology]. We [Gallup] will continue to do our part to contribute both financial and methodological resources to help harden with math and economics what many perceive to be a science that is too soft. They are of course, wrong, and have no idea of the power in many of the discoveries that you [Positive Psychological researchers] have made. The best partnership Gallup can have with this new institution is to help provide research and evidence that this science is as hard as physics or medicine. That will be our contribution (Clifton, 2002).

IS THE CLIFTON STRENGTHSFINDER SUPPOSED TO BE A WORK-RELATED INVENTORY, A CLINICAL INVENTORY, BOTH, OR NEITHER?

The Clifton StrengthsFinder is an omnibus assessment based on Positive Psychology. Its main application has been in the work domain, but it has been used for understanding individuals in a variety of settings — employees, executive teams, students, families, and personal development. It is *not* intended for clinical assessment or diagnosis of psychiatric disorders.

WHY ISN'T THE CLIFTON STRENGTHSFINDER BASED ON THE "BIG FIVE" FACTORS OF PERSONALITY THAT HAVE BEEN WELL ESTABLISHED IN RESEARCH JOURNALS SINCE THE 1980s?

The "big five" factors of personality are neuroticism (which reflects emotional stability — reverse-scored), extroversion (seeking the company of others), openness (interest in new experiences, ideas, and so forth), agreeableness (likeability, harmoniousness), and conscientiousness (rule abidance, discipline, integrity). A substantial amount of scientific research has demonstrated that human personality functioning can be summarized in terms of these five dimensions. This research has been conducted across cultures and languages (for example, McCrae and Costa, 1987; McCrae, Costa, Lima, et al., 1999; McCrae, Costa, Ostendorf, et al., 2000).

The major reason that the Clifton StrengthsFinder not based on the big five is that the big five is a measurement model rather than a conceptual one. It was derived from factor analysis. No theory underpinned it. It consists of the most generally agreed upon minimal number of personality factors, but conceptually it is no more correct than a model with four or six factors (Block, 1995; Hogan, Hogan, and Roberts, 1996). Some parts of the Clifton StrengthsFinder could be boiled down to aspects of the big five, but nothing would be gained from doing so. In fact, reducing the respondent's Clifton StrengthsFinder score to five dimensions would produce less information than is produced by any current measure of the big five since those measures also report subscores in addition to the five major dimensions.

HOW WAS THE CLIFTON STRENGTHSFINDER DEVELOPED?

The conceptual basis of the Clifton StrengthsFinder is grounded in over three decades of studying success across a wide variety of functions in business and education. Data from more than two million individuals were considered in the development of the Clifton StrengthsFinder. The item pairs were selected from a database of criterion-related validity studies, including over 100 predictive validity studies (Schmidt & Rader, 1999). Factor and reliability analyses were conducted in multiple samples to assess the contribution of items to measurement of themes and the consistency and stability of theme scores – thereby achieving the goal of a balance between maximized theme information and efficiency in instrument length.

WHY DOES THE CLIFTON STRENGTHSFINDER USE THESE 180 ITEM PAIRS AND NOT OTHERS?

These pairs reflect Gallup's research over three decades of studying successful people in a systematic, structured manner. They were derived from a quantitative review of item functioning, from a content review of the representativeness of themes and items within themes, with an eye toward the construct validity of the entire assessment. Given the breadth of talent we wish to assess, the pool of items is large and diverse. Well-known personality assessments range from 150 to upward of 400 items.

ARE THE CLIFTON STRENGTHSFINDER ITEMS IPSATIVELY SCORED, AND IF SO, DOES THIS LIMIT SCORING OF THE ITEMS?

Ipsativity is a mathematical term that refers to an aspect of a data matrix, such as a set of scores. A data matrix is said to be ipsative when the sum of the scores for each respondent is a constant. More generally, ipsativity refers to a set of scores that define a person in particular but is comparable between persons only in a very limited way. For example, if you rank-ordered your favorite colors and someone else rank-ordered their favorite colors, one could not compare the *intensity* of preference for any particular color due to ipsativity; only the *ranking* could be compared. Of the 180 Clifton StrengthsFinder items, less than 30 percent are ipsatively scored. These items are distributed over the range of Clifton StrengthsFinder themes, and no one theme contains more than one item scored in a way that would produce an ipsative data matrix (Plake, 1999).

HOW ARE CLIFTON STRENGTHSFINDER THEME SCORES CALCULATED?

Scores are calculated based on the mean of the intensity of self-description. The respondent is given three response options for each self-description: strongly agree, agree, and neutral. A proprietary formula assigns a value to each response category. Values for items in the theme are averaged to derive a theme score. Scores can be reported as a mean, as a standard score, or as a percentile.

WAS MODERN TEST SCORE THEORY (FOR EXAMPLE, IRT) USED TO DEVELOP THE CLIFTON STRENGTHSFINDER?

The Clifton StrengthsFinder was developed to capitalize on the accumulated knowledge and experience of Gallup's talent-based strengths practice. Thus, items were initially chosen on the basis of traditional validity evidence (construct, content, criterion). This is a universally accepted method for developing assessments. Methods to apply IRT to assessments that are both heterogeneous and homogeneous are only now being explored (for example, Waller, Thompson, and Wenk, 2000). Further iterations of the Clifton StrengthsFinder may well use other statistical methods to refine the instrument.

WHAT CONSTRUCT VALIDITY RESEARCH HAS BEEN CONDUCTED IN RELATION TO THE CLIFTON STRENGTHSFINDER?

The Clifton StrengthsFinder is an omnibus assessment of talents based on Positive Psychology. Therefore, it undoubtedly has correlational linkages to these measures to about the same extent that personality measures link to other measures in general.

Construct validity can be assessed through a number of analysis types. During development phases, a number of items were pilot tested. The items with the strongest psychometric properties (including item correlation to theme) were retained.

Items should correlate to their proposed themes (constructs) at a higher level than they do to other themes (constructs.) In a follow-up study of 601,049 respondents, the average item-to-proposed-theme correlation (corrected for part-whole overlap) was 6.6 times larger than the average item correlation to other themes.

Construct validity can also be assessed on the basis of convergent and discriminant validity evidence. A 2003 construct validity study explored the relationship between the Clifton StrengthsFinder and the five-factor model of personality. Several expected associations between Clifton StrengthsFinder themes and five-factor model constructs were found. For example, the Discipline theme correlates .81 with a measure of conscientiousness. Theoretically, these constructs have similar definition in relation to orderliness and planning. Other examples include the .83 correlation between Woo and extroversion, the .70 correlation between Ideation and intellectence, and the .58 correlation between Positivity and agreeableness.

Convergent and discriminant validity studies are a part of past and ongoing construct validity research.

CAN CLIFTON STRENGTHSFINDER SCORES CHANGE?

This is an important question for which there are both technical and conceptual answers.

Technical answers: The talents measured by Clifton StrengthsFinder are expected to demonstrate a property called reliability. Reliability has several definitions. The most important form of reliability estimate for the Clifton StrengthsFinder is technically known as test-retest reliability, which is the extent to which scores are stable over time. Test-retest reliabilities on the Clifton StrengthsFinder themes are high, relative to current psychometric standards.

Almost all Clifton StrengthsFinder themes have a test-retest reliability over a six-month interval between .60 and .80. A maximum test-retest reliability score of 1 would indicate that all Clifton StrengthsFinder respondents received *exactly* the same score over two assessments. The average correlation of an individual's theme ranking across multiple time periods is .74 (across 706 participants with an average of 17 months between administrations).

Conceptual answers: While an evaluation of the full extent of this stability is, of course, an empirical question, the conceptual origins of a person's talents are also relevant. Gallup has studied the life themes of top performers in an extensive series of research studies combining qualitative and quantitative investigations over many years. Participants have included youths in their early teens to adults in their mid-seventies. In each of these studies, the focal point was the identification of long-standing patterns of thought, feeling, and behavior associated with success. The lines of interview questioning used were both prospective and retrospective, such as "What do you want to be doing ten years from now?" and "At what age did you make your first sale?" In other words, the timeframe of interest in our original studies of excellence in job performance was long term, not short term. Many of the items developed provided useful predictions of job stability, thereby suggesting that the measured attributes were of a persistent nature. Tracking studies of job performance over two- to three-year time spans added to the Gallup understanding of what it takes for a job incumbent to be consistently effective, rather than just achieving impressive short-term gains. The prominence of dimensions and items relating to motivation and to values in much of the original life themes research also informed the design of a Clifton StrengthsFinder instrument that can identify those enduring human qualities.

At this relatively early stage in the application of the Clifton StrengthsFinder, it is not yet clear how long an individual's salient features, so measured, will endure. In general, however, it is likely to be years rather than months. We may perhaps project a minimum of five years and upper ranges of 30 to 40 years and longer. There is growing evidence (for example, Judge, Higgins, Thoresen, and Barrick, 1999) that some aspects of personality are predictive throughout many decades of the life span. Some Clifton StrengthsFinder themes may turn out to be more enduring than others. Cross-sectional studies of different age groups will provide the earliest insights into possible age-related changes in normative patterns of behaviors. The first explanations for apparent changes in themes, as measured, should therefore be sought in the direction of measurement error rather than as indications of a true change in the underlying trait, emotion, or cognition. The respondents themselves should also be invited to offer an explanation for any apparent discrepancies.

HOW CAN ONE DETERMINE THAT THE CLIFTON STRENGTHSFINDER WORKS?

Whether an assessment such as the Clifton StrengthsFinder "works" is part of an ongoing study of the construct validity of the instrument through psychometric and conceptual review. The Clifton StrengthsFinder is based on more than 30 years' of evidence on the nature of talents and the application of strengths analysis. This evidence was summarized in a recent scientific study that used meta-analysis (Schmidt & Rader, 1999).

The research literature in the behavioral and social sciences includes a multitude of individual studies with apparently conflicting conclusions. Meta-analysis allows the researcher to estimate the mean correlation between variables and make corrections for artifactual sources of variation in findings across studies. As such, it provides uniquely powerful information because it controls for measurement and sampling errors and other idiosyncrasies that distort the results of individual studies. (More than one thousand meta-analyses have been published in the psychological, educational, behavioral, medical, and personnel selection fields.) For a detailed review of meta-analysis across a variety of fields, see Lipsey and Wilson (1993).

WHAT IS STRENGTHS-BASED DEVELOPMENT?

Strengths-based development is a process that increases an individual's ability to consistently perform a specific task at a nearly perfect level. A strength is made up of skills, knowledge, and talents. Skills are one's basic abilities to perform the steps of specific tasks, such as the ability to operate a computer. Skills do not naturally exist within us; they must be acquired through training and practice. Knowledge, defined simply as what you know, includes facts (factual knowledge) and understandings (gained through experience) that can be productively applied to specific tasks. Knowledge does not naturally exist within us; it must be acquired. Talents are recurring patterns of thought, feeling, or behavior that can be productively applied to specific tasks, such as the inner drive to compete, sensitivity to the needs of others, and the tendency to be outgoing at social gatherings. Although talents cannot be acquired, we each have talents that naturally exist within us — and because those talents represent the best of our natural selves, they are the crucial component of strengths and our best opportunities to perform at levels of excellence.

Identification of talent is critical to strengths-based development. A popular means for identifying talent is to consider an individual's top five areas of talent as indicated by responses to the Clifton StrengthsFinder, Gallup's online talent assessment instrument. Considering these top five areas ("themes") of talent, known as one's Signature Themes, can help individuals understand and, as a result, internalize the themes that offer their most natural talents.

Signature Themes are a useful resource in the identification of talent. One's spontaneous reactions to any situation are an important indicator of talents, and the ranking of themes presented in a Clifton StrengthsFinder report is based upon spontaneous, top-of-mind reactions to the paired descriptors presented by the instrument.

Yearnings, rapid learning, satisfactions, and timelessness should also be considered when identifying talents (Clifton & Nelson, 1992). Yearnings reveal the presence of a talent, particularly when they are felt early in life. A yearning can be described as a pull, a magnetic influence, which draws one to a particular activity or environment time and again. Rapid learning offers another trace of talent. In the context of a new challenge or a new environment, something sparks in individual's talent. Immediately their brain seems to light up as if a whole bank of switches were suddenly flicked to "on" — and the speed at which they learn a new skill or gain new knowledge provides a telltale clue to the talent's presence and power. Satisfactions are psychological fulfillment that results when one takes on and successfully meets challenges that engage their greatest talents. Timelessness can also serve as a clue to talent. When individuals become so engrossed in an activity that they lose track of time, it may be because the activity engaged one of their talents.

Strengths-based development begins with the identification of talent, and continues as one integrates their talents into their view of self. Successful strengths-based development results in desired behavioral change (Clifton & Harter, 2003). Client-sponsored studies have provided evidence that strengths-based development relates to various positive outcomes, including increases in employee engagement and productivity.

Managers who create environments in which employees are able to make the most of their talents have more productive work units with less employee turnover (Clifton & Harter, 2003). Studies show that strengths-based development increases self-confidence, direction, hope, and altruism (Hodges & Clifton, 2004). Ongoing research continues to explore the impact of strengths-based development on desired outcomes.

HOW CAN THE CLIFTON STRENGTHSFINDER BE ADMINISTERED, SCORED, AND REPORTED FOR INDIVIDUALS WHO ARE UNABLE TO USE THE INTERNET BECAUSE OF EITHER DISABILITY OR ECONOMIC STATUS?

In regard to economic status (a.k.a. the digital divide), possible solutions include accessing the Internet from a library or school. It should be noted that some organizations that Gallup works with do not have universal Internet access. In these cases, as with those from disadvantaged backgrounds, the solution generally has involved special access from a few central locations.

In regard to disability, a range of accommodations is available. Generally, the most effective is for the participant to request that the timer that governs the pace of the Clifton StrengthsFinder administration be turned off. This and other accommodations would need to be arranged with Gallup on a case-by-case basis in advance of taking the Clifton StrengthsFinder.

WHAT IS THE RECOMMENDED READING LEVEL FOR CLIFTON STRENGTHSFINDER USERS? WHAT ALTERNATIVES ARE AVAILABLE FOR THOSE WHO DO NOT MEET THAT LEVEL?

The Clifton StrengthsFinder is designed for completion by those with at least an eighth- to tenth-grade reading level (in most cases, those 14 years of age or older). Trials of the Clifton StrengthsFinder in our youth leadership studies have demonstrated neither significant nor consistent problems in completion of the Clifton StrengthsFinder by teens. Possible alternatives or accommodations include turning off the pace timer to allow time to consult a dictionary or otherwise ask about the meaning of a word.

IS THE CLIFTON STRENGTHSFINDER APPROPRIATE ACROSS DEMOGRAPHIC GROUPS, COUNTRIES, AND LANGUAGES?

There is overwhelming evidence from both Gallup and other research organizations that the structure of talent and personality dimensions such as those measured by the Clifton StrengthsFinder and other instruments do not vary across cultures and nationalities.

For instance, the average item-to-theme correlation is quite similar across countries. The standard deviation of the correlations across countries is .026 and ranges from .01 to .04 across themes. Across languages, similar results were obtained, with an average standard deviation of the correlations across languages of .024 and range from .01 to .03. With regard to theme intercorrelations, the standard deviation across countries averaged .03 with range of .01 to .07 across the 561 theme intercorrelations. Across languages, the standard deviation averaged .02, with range from .01 to .06. In summary, the theme intercorrelations are stable across cultural contexts.

The Clifton StrengthsFinder has international presence as a talent measurement instrument. It is currently available in 17 languages, with several other translations planned for the future. More than 110,000 of the first one million respondents completed the Clifton StrengthsFinder in a language other than English. Clifton StrengthsFinder respondents have come from nearly 50 different countries. Twenty-five of these countries have had at least 1,000 respondents. More than 225,000 respondents report a country of residence other than the United States.

Research exploring the age of Clifton StrengthsFinder respondents has revealed that the average item-to-theme correlation is quite similar across age groups. Average standard deviation of the correlations is .02 and ranges from .00 to .09 across themes.

Research into the gender of Clifton StrengthsFinder respondents has revealed that the item-total correlations are similar and consistently positive. Differences in item-total correlations between genders range from .00 to .06 across themes.

WHAT FEEDBACK DOES A RESPONDENT GET FROM THE CLIFTON STRENGTHSFINDER?

Feedback varies in accordance with the reason the person completes the Clifton StrengthsFinder. Sometimes the respondent receives only a report listing his or her top five themes — those in which the person received his or her highest scores. In other situations the person may also review the remaining 29 themes, along with action suggestions for each theme, in a personal feedback session with a Gallup consultant or in a supervised team-building session with their colleagues.

Theme combinations are rare and powerful. There are 278,256 possible unique combinations of Signature Themes, and 33.39 million different permutations with unique order can exist.

Since 1998, the Clifton StrengthsFinder has been used as Gallup's initial diagnostic tool in development programs with various academic institutions, faith-based organizations, major businesses, and other organizations. The Clifton StrengthsFinder has been used to facilitate the development of individuals across hundreds of roles including: manager, customer service representative, salesperson, administrative assistant, nurse, lawyer, pastor, leader, student, teacher, and school administrator.

REFERENCES

The following references are provided for those readers interested in particular details of this technical report. This reference list is not meant to be exhaustive, and although many of the references use advanced statistical techniques, the reader should not be deterred from reviewing them.

American Educational Research Association, American Psychological Association, National Council on Measurement in Education (AERA/APA/NCME). 1999. *Standards for educational and psychological testing.* Washington, D.C.: American Educational Research Association.

American Psychologist. Positive psychology [special issue]. 2000. Washington, D.C.: American Psychological Association.

Block, J. 1995. A contrarian view of the five-factor approach to personality description. Psychological Bulletin *117:187–215.*

Cameron, K.S., Dutton, J.E., & Quinn, R.E. (Eds.). 2003. *Positive organizational scholarship.* San Francisco: Berrett-Koehler.

Clifton, D.O., & Harter, J.K. 2003. Strengths investment. In K.S. Cameron, J.E. Dutton, & R.E. Quinn (Eds.), *Positive organizational scholarship.* (pp. 111-121). San Francisco: Berrett-Koehler.

Clifton, D.O, & Nelson, P. 1992. Soar with your strengths. New York: Delacorte Press.

Clifton, J.K. 2002. Letter addressed to attendees of the first international Positive Psychology Summit, Washington, DC.

Hodges, T.D., & Clifton, D.O. 2004. Strengths-based development in practice. In A. Linley & S. Joseph (Eds.), Handbook of positive psychology in practice. *Hoboken, New Jersey: John Wiley and Sons, Inc.*

Hogan, R., J. Hogan, and B. W. Roberts. 1996. Personality measurement and employment decisions: Questions and answers. American Psychologist *51:469–77.*

Hunter, J. E., and F. L. Schmidt. 1990. Methods of meta-analysis: Correcting error and bias in research findings. *Newbury Park, CA: Sage.*

Judge, T. A., C. A. Higgins, C. J. Thoresen, and M. R. Barrick. 1999. The big five personality traits, general mental ability, and career success across the life span. Personnel Psychology *52:621–52.*

Keyes, C.L.M., & Haidt, J. (Eds.). 2003. *Flourishing: Positive psychology and the life well-lived.* Washington, DC: APA.

Linley, A., & Joseph, S. (Eds.). 2004. Positive psychology in practice. *Hoboken, NJ: John Wiley & Sons, Inc.*

Lipsey, M. W., and D. B. Wilson. 1993. The efficacy of psychological, educational, and behavioral treatment. American Psychologist *48:1181–1209.*

Lopez, S.J., & Snyder, C.R. (Eds.). 2003. Positive psychological assessment: A handbook of models and measures. *Washington, DC: American Psychological Association.*

McCrae, R. R., and P. T. Costa. 1987. Validation of the five-factor model of personality across instruments and observers. Journal of Personality and Social Psychology *52:81–90.*

McCrae, R. R., P. T. Costa, M. P. de Lima, et al. 1999. Age differences in personality across the adult life span: Parallels in five cultures. Developmental Psychology *35:466–77.*

McCrae, R. R., P. T. Costa, F. Ostendorf, et al. 2000. Nature over nurture: Temperament, personality, and life span development. Journal of Personality and Social Psychology *78:173–86.*

Myers, D. 2000. The funds, friends, and faith of happy people. American Psychologist, *55: 56-67.*

Plake, B. 1999. An investigation of ipsativity and multicollinearity properties of the StrengthsFinder Instrument *[technical report]. Lincoln, NE: The Gallup Organization.*

Schmidt, F.L., & Rader, M. 1999. Exploring the boundary conditions for interview validity: Meta-analytic validity findings for a new interview type. *Personnel Psychology,* 52: 445-464.

Sheldon, K., Fredrickson, B., Rathunde, K., & Csikszentmihalyi, M. 2000. Positive psychology manifesto (Rev. Ed.). Philadelphia. Retrieved May 1, 2003 from the World Wide Web: http://www.positivepsychology.org/akumalmanifesto.htm.

Snyder, C.R., & Lopez, S.J. (Eds.). 2002. The handbook of positive psychology. *New York: Oxford University Press.*

Waller, N. G., J. S. Thompson, and E. Wenk. 2000. Using IRT to separate measurement bias from true group differences on homogeneous and heterogeneous scales: An illustration with the MMPI. Psychological Methods *5:125–46.*

ACKNOWLEDGEMENTS

There are so many individuals who helped make this book a reality, and we owe them a great debt of gratitude.

Many thanks to Jim Clifton, Gallup's chairman and CEO, whose vision of influencing every single world leader with Gallup's discoveries led to the creation of the Faith Communities Practice. Without his commitment to that vision, this book would never have happened.

Thank you to Larry Emond and Evan Perkins for their support, encouragement, and insight; to Geoff Brewer, one of the most talented editors on the planet; to the editing and proofing team of Paul Petters, Mark Stiemann, and Kelly Henry, whose talents for attention to detail were invaluable. Dennis Welch, Scott Simmons, and Cinda Hicks helped us keep the needs of the market clearly in mind. Tom Rath and Piotrek Juszkiewicz were superb managers and always made sure that the project was on track and on schedule. Chin-Yee Lai designed the book's excellent and compelling cover, and Kim Simeon and Mary Gansemer produced the attractive and easy-to-read layout.

A host of other Gallup associates also made significant contributions to the *Living Your Strengths* project. They include Sherry Ehrlich, Irene Burklund, Wyn Sipple, Lori Stohs, Jerry Krueger, Kryste Wiedenfeld, Rosemary Travis, Jim Harter, Tim Hodges, Julie Hawkins, Sue Munn, Tonya Fredstrom, and Robin Seals.

Finally and most importantly, we express our deepest gratitude to our wives, Jane Winseman, Shirley Clifton, and Rosanne Liesveld, and our children, who supported and encouraged us throughout the process.

For more information about how to put the power of *Living Your Strengths* to work in your church, please call (402) 938-6304 or check out our Web site at http://gallupfaith.com.

If you'd like to contact us via e-mail, or share with us how your congregation is making the most of its talents through strengths development, please contact us at lys@gallup.com.

To keep up-to-date on Gallup's latest discoveries in congregational engagement, read the Religion & Social Trends articles at www.galluppoll.com.

Gallup Press exists to educate and inform the people who govern, manage, teach, and lead the world's six billion citizens. Each book meets The Gallup Organization's requirements of integrity, trust, and independence and is based on Gallup-approved science and research.